RECORDED VERSIONS
GUITAR

AUTHENTIC TRANSCRIPTIONS
WITH NOTES AND TABLATURE

TODAY'S FOLK★ROCK HITS

ISBN 978-1-4803-9622-7

HAL•LEONARD®
CORPORATION

7777 W. BLUEMOUND RD. P.O. BOX 13819 MILWAUKEE, WI 53213

Visit Hal Leonard Online at
www.halleonard.com

from *Magpie and the Dandelion*

Another Is Waiting

Words and Music by Scott Avett, Timothy Avett and Robert Crawford

Gtr. 1 tuning:
(low to high) E-A-D-G-B-D

*Banjo arr. for gtr.

**Chord symbols reflect overall harmony.

C

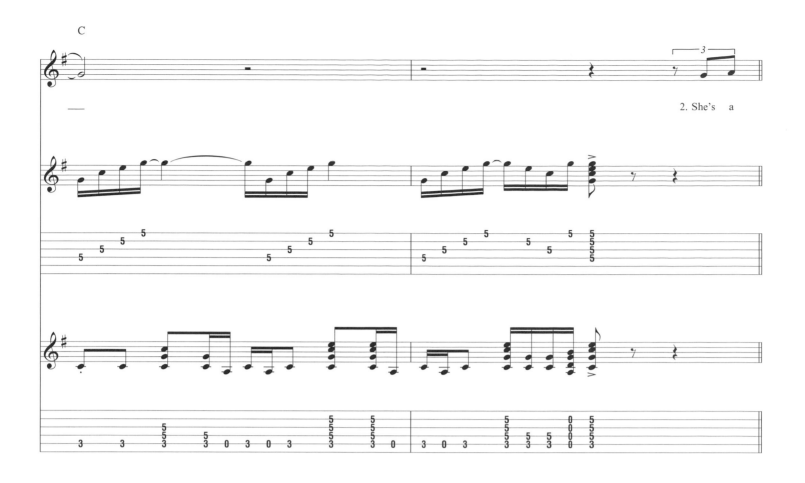

2. She's a

Verse

G   Em   Bm   D

rose,   she's a queen.   But she's star - ing at___ a mag - a - zine___ in the dark.___

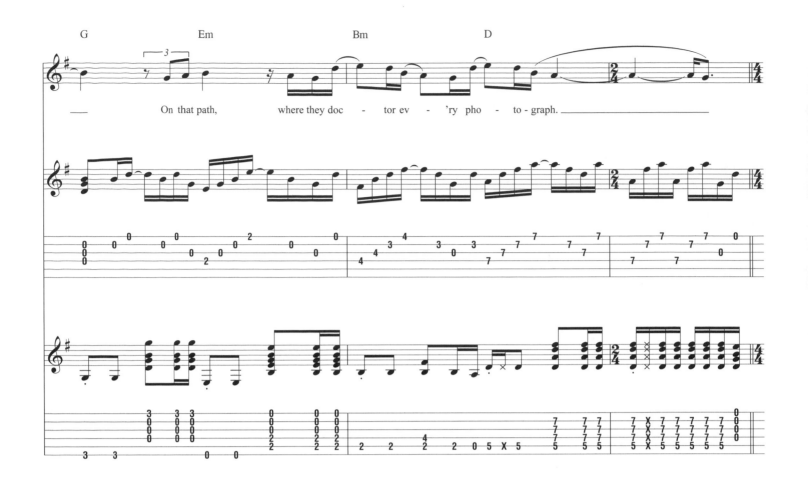

On that path,   where they doc - tor ev - 'ry pho - to - graph.

Chorus

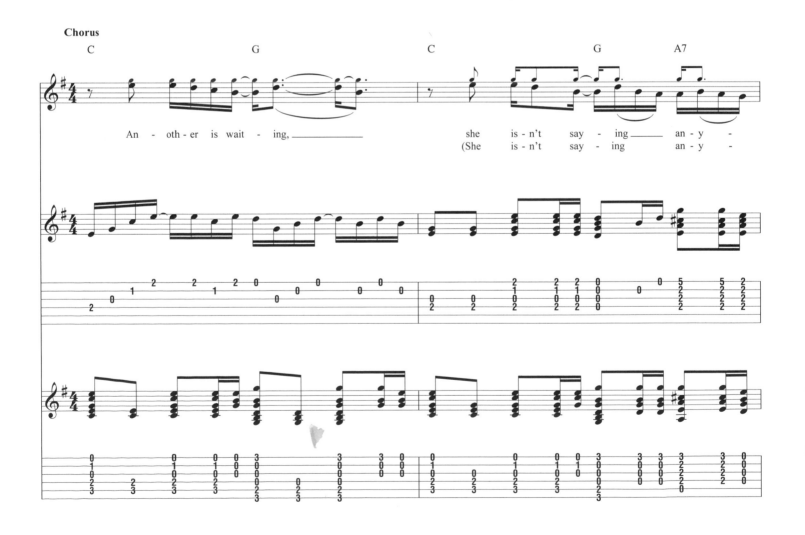

An - oth - er is wait - ing,   she   is - n't   say - ing   an - y -
(She   is - n't   say - ing   an - y -

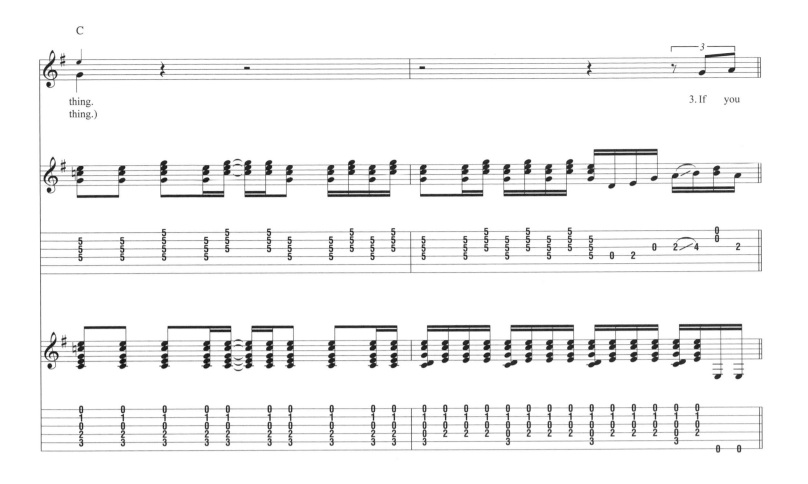

thing.
thing.)

3. If you

Verse

care, if you like, well, I'm stand - ing in ___ the lan - tern light. ___ With our

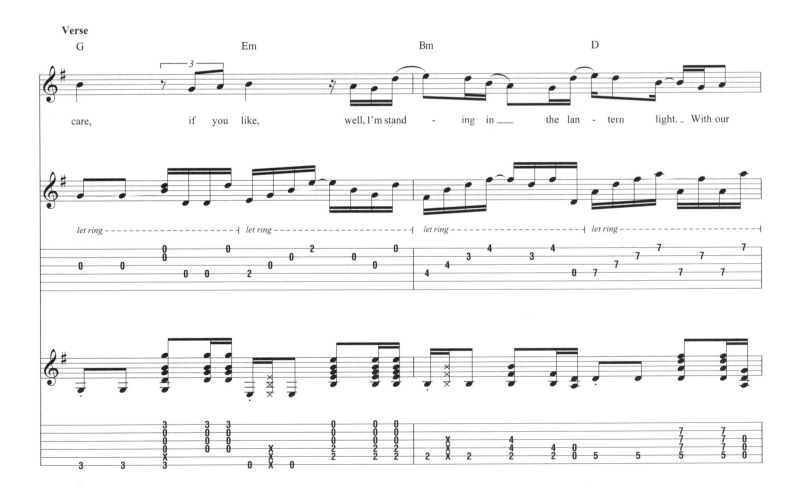

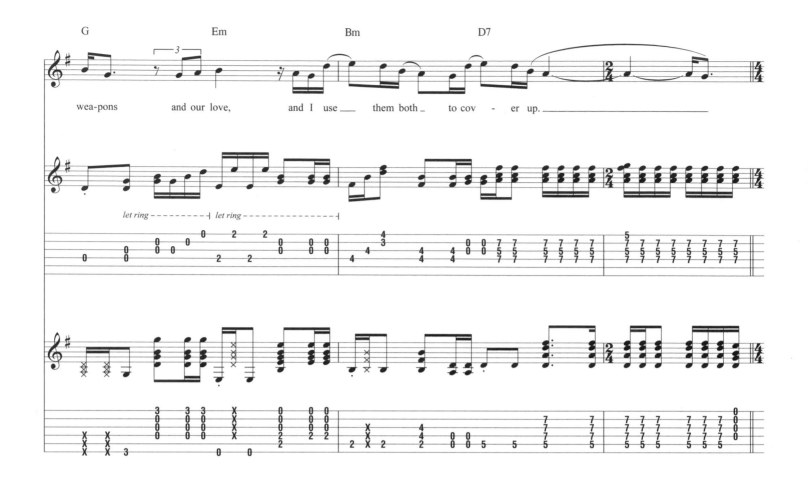

weap-ons   and our love,   and I use____ them both__ to cov - er up.____

Chorus

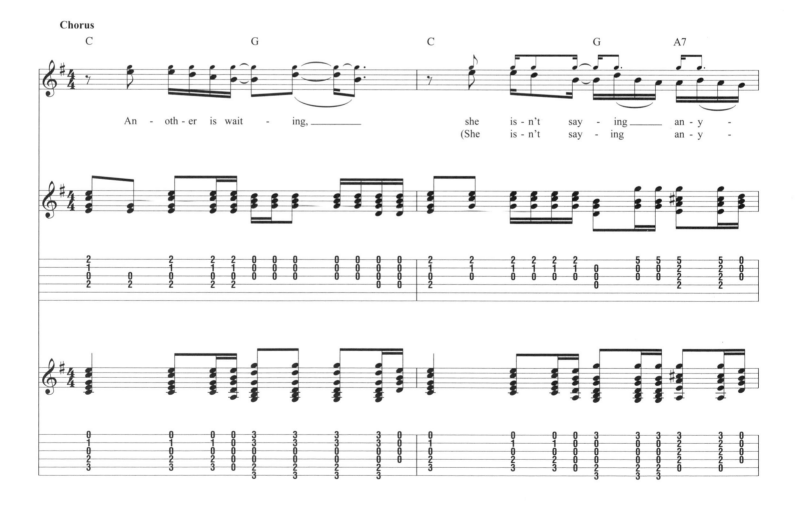

An - oth-er is wait - ing,_____   she is - n't say - ing___ an - y -
(She is - n't say - ing an - y -

If I could, ___ I would come ___ right in ___ and take ___ you ___ off ___ my - self. ___

4. It's a

Verse

G | **Em** | Gtr. 4 tacet **Bm** | **D**

fake, it's a con, the na-ture of____ the road____ you're on,____ let me

G | **Em** | **Bm** | **D7**

see your skel-e-ton, well be-fore____ your life____ is done.____

Gtr. 1

Gtr. 2

Gtr. 3

She is-n't say - ing _____ an - y - thing.
(She is-n't say - ing _____ an - y - thing.)

from Of Monsters and Men - *My Head Is an Animal*

Dirty Paws

Words and Music by Of Monsters And Men

Gtrs. 1 & 4: Capo III

*Symbols in parentheses represent chord names respective to capoed guitar.
Symbols above reflect actual sounding chords.
Capoed fret is "0" in tab. Chord symbols reflect implied harmony.

Verse

1. Jump-ing up and down the floor, ___ my head ___ is an an - i - mal. ___ And

**Bkgd. Voc. is female & sounds one octave lower than written throughout.

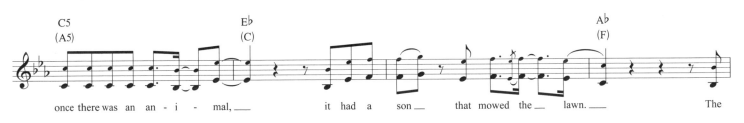

once there was an an - i - mal, ___ it had a son ___ that mowed the ___ lawn. ___ The

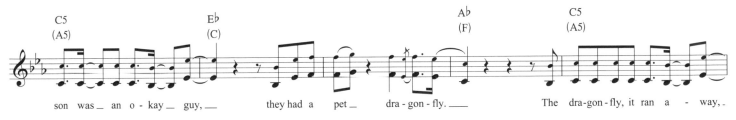

son was ___ an o - kay guy, ___ they had a pet ___ dra - gon - fly. ___ The dra-gon-fly, it ran a - way, ___

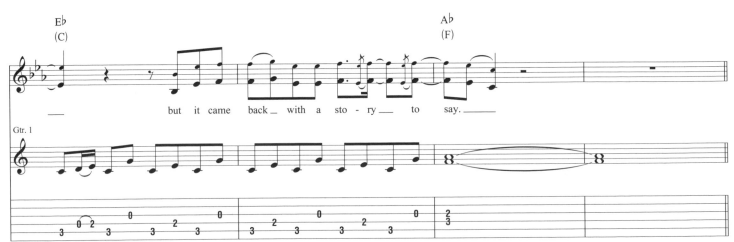

but it came back ___ with a sto - ry ___ to say. ___

birds, they got help from be-low, ___ from dirt-y paws ___ and the crea-tures ___ of ___ snow.

Chorus

Interlude

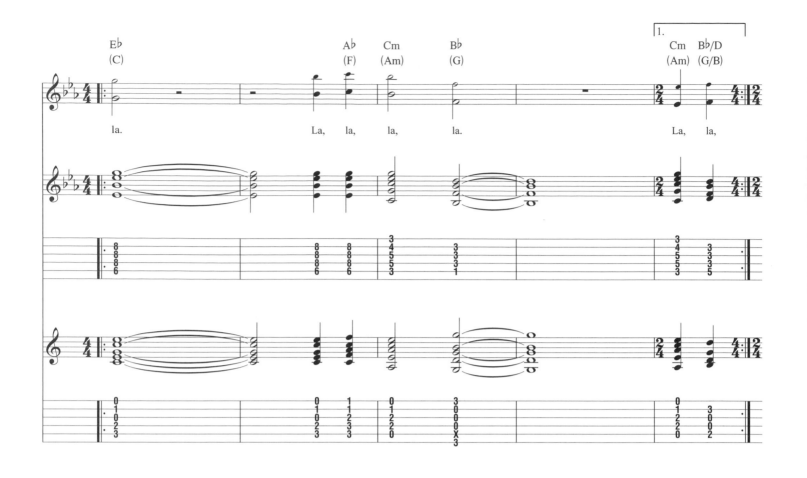

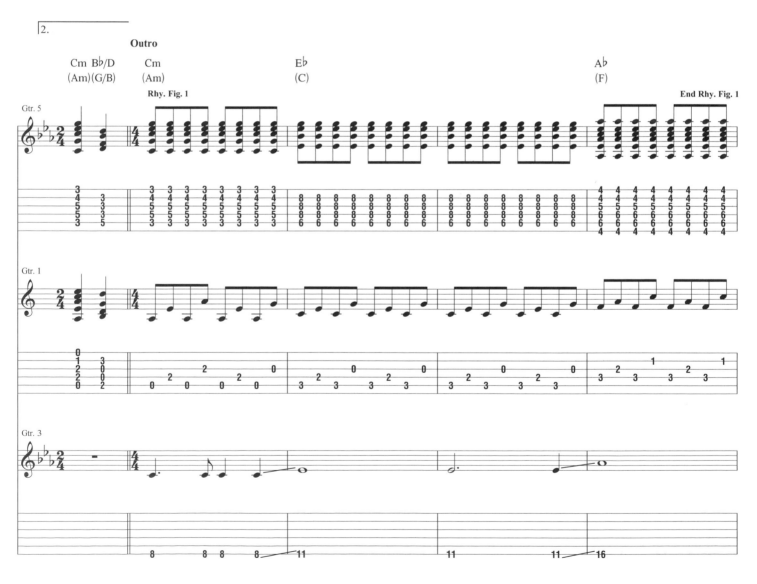

5 Years Time

By Charlie Fink

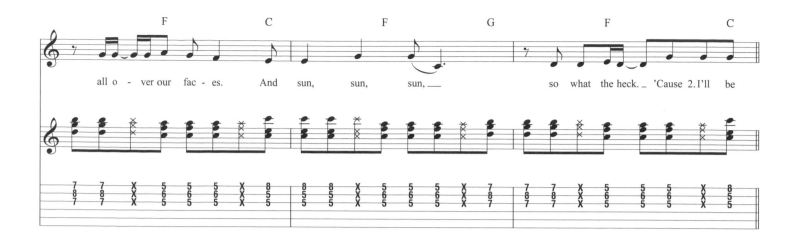

all o - ver our fac - es. And sun, sun, sun, ___ so what the heck. ___ 'Cause 2.I'll be

Verse

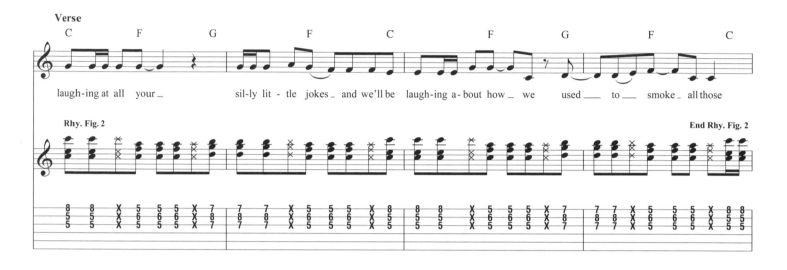

laugh-ing at all your ___ sil-ly lit - tle jokes ___ and we'll be laugh-ing a - bout how ___ we used ___ to ___ smoke ___ all those

Rhy. Fig. 2   End Rhy. Fig. 2

Gtr. 3: w/ Rhy. Fig. 2

stu - pid lit - tle cig - a - rettes and drink stu - pid wine. ___ 'Cause it's what we ___ need - ed to have a good time. ___ But it was

*Bkgd. Voc. is female & sounds one octave lower than written, next 2 meas.

Chorus

Gtr. 3: w/ Rhy. Fig. 2 (1 1/4 times)

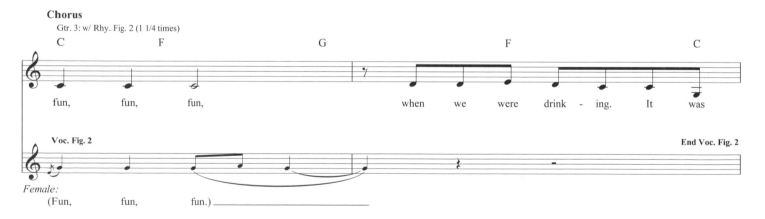

fun, fun, fun, when we were drink - ing. It was

Voc. Fig. 2   End Voc. Fig. 2

Female:
(Fun, fun, fun.) _____

Bkgd. Voc.: w/ Voc. Fig. 2 (3 times)

fun, fun, fun, when we were drunk. ___ And it was fun, fun, fun, ___

when we were laugh - ing. It was fun, fun, fun. ___ Oh, it was fun. ___

Gtr. 3

Interlude

Gtr. 3: w/ Rhy. Fig. 2

3. Oh, well I'll

Verse

Gtr. 3: w/ Rhy. Fig. 3 (2 times)

look at you and say it's the hap - pi - est that I've ev - er been ___ and I'll say, "I no long - er feel ___ I have to be ___

___ James Dean." ___ And she'll say, "Yeah, well I feel, oh, pret - ty hap - py, too." ___ And I'm al -

*Bkgd. voc. female, as before.

**Bkgd. voc. male, next 3 meas.

Chorus

Gtr. 3: w/ Rhy. Fig. 1 (1st 2 meas., 2 times)

ways pret - ty hap - py when I'm ___ just kick - ing back ___ with you. And it be love, love, love, all through our bod - ies. And

Voc. Fig. 3

End Voc. Fig. 3

Female: (Love, love, love.) _____

Bkgd. Voc.: w/ Voc. Fig. 3 (3 times)

Gtr. 3: w/ Rhy. Fig. 1

love, love, love, all through our minds ___ and it be love, love, love, ___

all o - ver her ___ face. And love, love, love, ___ all o - ver mine. ___ 4. And though ad -

Verse

Gtr. 3 tacet

C　　　　F　　　　G　　　　F　　　　C

mit-ted-ly　all　those　mo-ments　are　just　in　my　head.＿＿　I'll be

Gtr. 1: w/ Riff A (3 times)

F　　G　　F　　C　　F　　G

think-ing 'bout＿ them＿ as I'm ly - ing in＿ bed.＿ And I know＿ that ad - mit-ted-ly they might not

F　　　　C　　　　F　　　　G　　　　F　　　　C

e - ven come＿ true＿ but in my mind I'm＿ hav - ing a pret-ty good　　time with　　you.＿ Oh,　in

*Bkgd. voc. male, next 3 meas.

Chorus

Gtr. 1: w/ Riff A (2 1/2 times)

C　　　　F　　　　G　　　　F　　　　C

five　　years　　time,　　　　　　　I　might　not　know　you.　　In

Female:

(Five　　years　　time.) ＿＿＿＿＿＿＿＿＿＿

Bkgd. Voc.: w/ Voc. Fig. 4 (3 times)

five years time   we might not speak. Oh,___ in   five   years   time,___

we might not get a-long.___ In five   years   time,___   you might just prove me

Gtr. 1: w/ Riff A
Gtr. 3 tacet

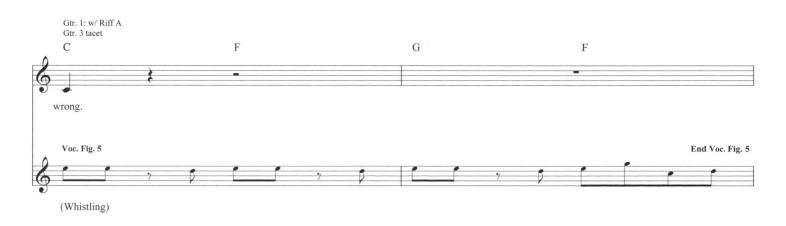

wrong.

Voc. Fig. 5   End Voc. Fig. 5

(Whistling)

Bkgd. Voc.: w/ Voc. Fig. 5 (4 1/2 times)

Oh, there'll be love, love, love,

Gtr. 1

Gtr. 1 tacet
N.C.

wher - ev - er you go. There'll be love, love, love, wher - ev - er you go. There'll be

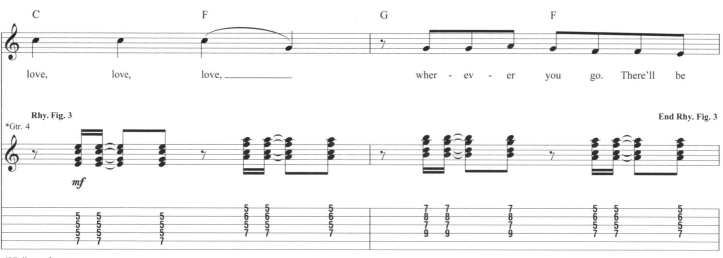

love, love, love, _____ wher - ev - er you go. There'll be

Rhy. Fig. 3
*Gtr. 4

End Rhy. Fig. 3

mf

*Violin arr. for gtr.

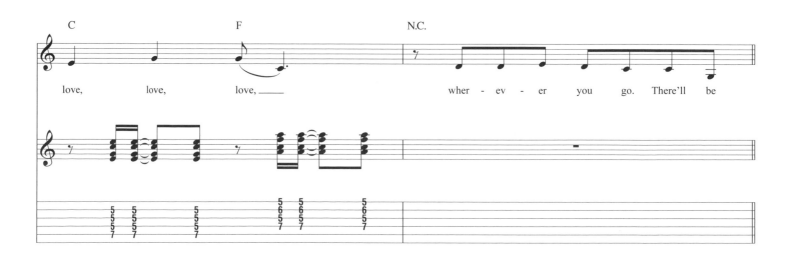

love, love, love, _____ wher - ev - er you go. There'll be

Bkgd. Voc.: w/ Voc. Fig. 3 (4 times)
Gtr. 4: w/ Rhy. Fig. 3 (3 times)

love,   love,   love,   wher - ev - er   you   go. There'll be   love,   love,   love,

Gtr. 3

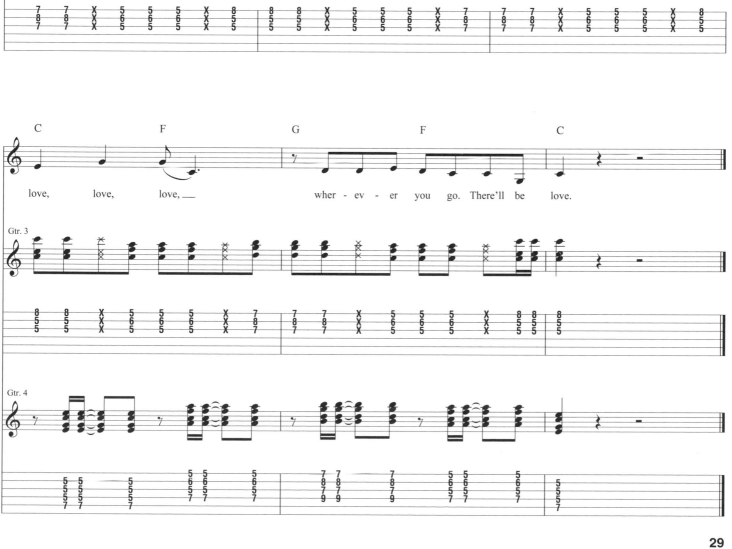

wher - ev - er   you   go. There'll be   love,   love,   love, _____   wher - ev - er   you   go. There'll be

love,   love,   love, __   wher - ev - er   you   go. There'll be   love.

Gtr. 3

Gtr. 4

from Phillip Phillips - *The World from the Side of the Moon*

Gone, Gone, Gone

Words and Music by Gregg Wattenberg, Derek Fuhrmann and Todd Clark

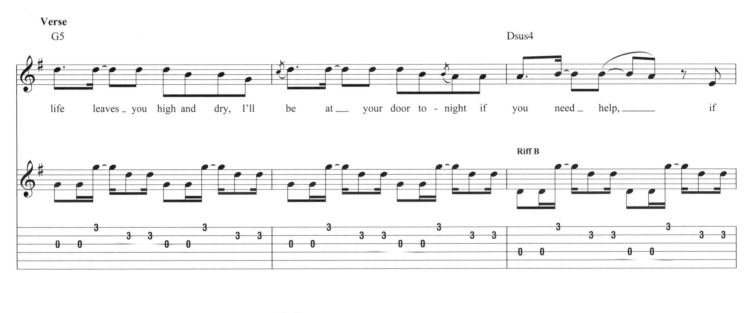

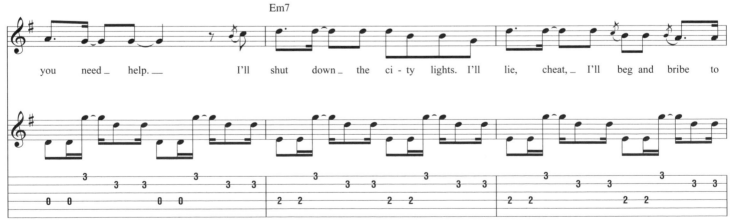

Csus2

make you well, to make you well. When

End Riff B

Gtr. 1: w/ Riff A

G5

en - e - mies are at your door, I'll car - ry you a - way from war if

Gtr. 1: w/ Riff B

Dsus4   Em7

you need help, if you need help. Your hope dang - lin' by a string, I'll

Csus2

share in your suf-fer-ing to make you well, to make you well. Give me

Pre-Chorus

C5   G   D5/A   C5   G   D5/A   N.C.

rea - sons to be - lieve that you would do the same for me. And I would do it for

Gtr. 1

slight P.M.

Verse

Gtr. 1: w/ Riff C

G5

fall like ___ a sta - tue, I'm gon - na be there ___ to catch you, put you

(Oo, _____

Gtr. 1: w/ Riff B

Dsus4   Em7

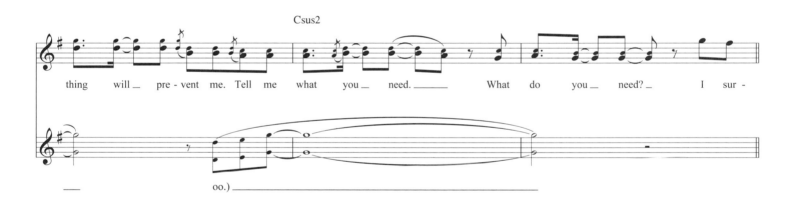

on your ___ feet, _____ you on your ___ feet. ___ And if your well ___ is emp - ty, not a

_____ oo, _____

Csus2

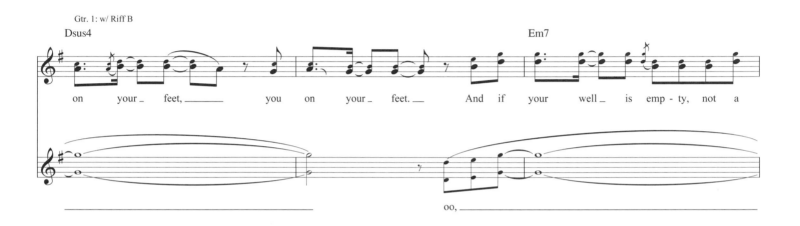

thing will ___ pre - vent me. Tell me what you ___ need. _____ What do you ___ need? ___ I sur -

___ oo.) _____

D.S. al Coda

Pre-Chorus

C5   G   D5/A   C5   G   D5/A   N.C.

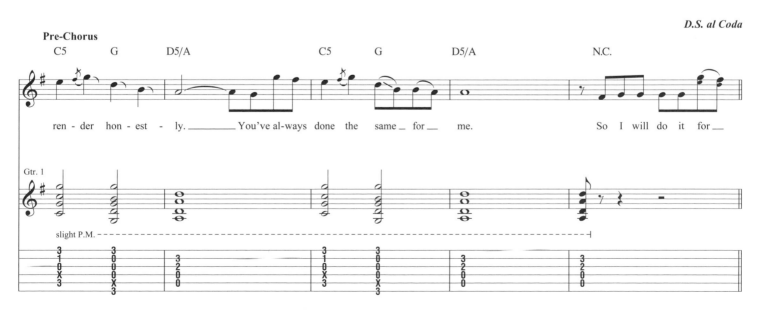

ren - der hon - est - ly. _____ You've al - ways done the same ___ for ___ me.   So I will do it for ___

Gtr. 1

slight P.M. - |

33

Coda

Bridge

Gtr. 2 tacet

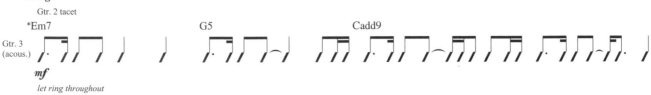

gone. You're my back - bone, ___ you're my cor-ner - stone. ___ You're my crutch when my legs stop mov - in'.

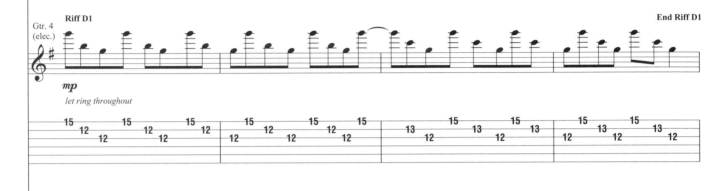

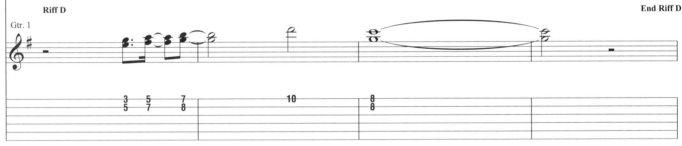

*See top of first page of song for chord diagrams pertaining to rhythm slashes.

Gtrs. 1 & 4: w/ Riffs D & D1
Gtr. 3 tacet

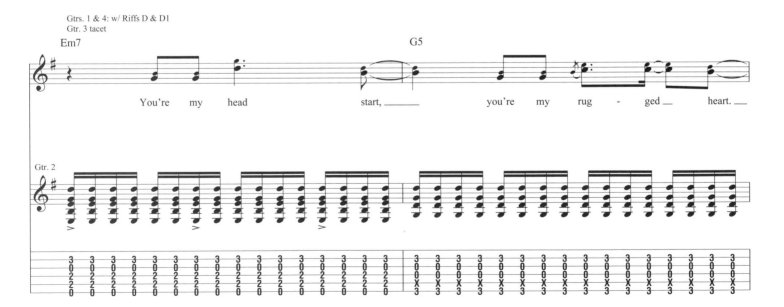

You're my head start, _____ you're my rug - ged ___ heart. ___

34

You're the pulse that I've al - ways ____ need - ed.

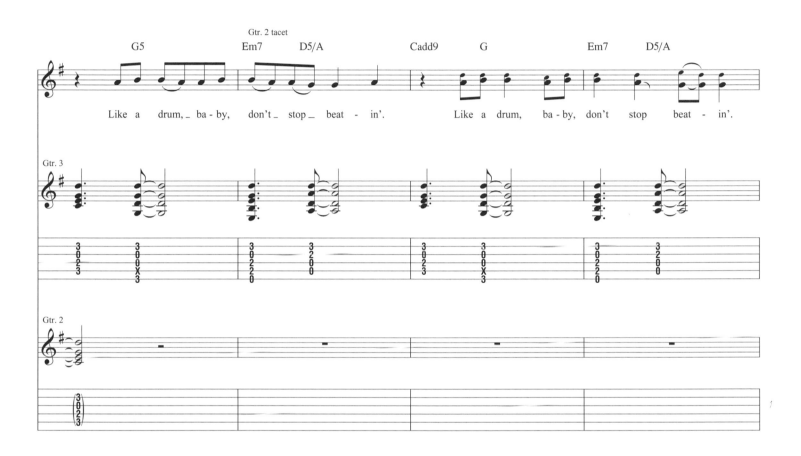

Like a drum, _ ba - by, don't _ stop _ beat - in'. Like a drum, ba - by, don't stop beat - in'.

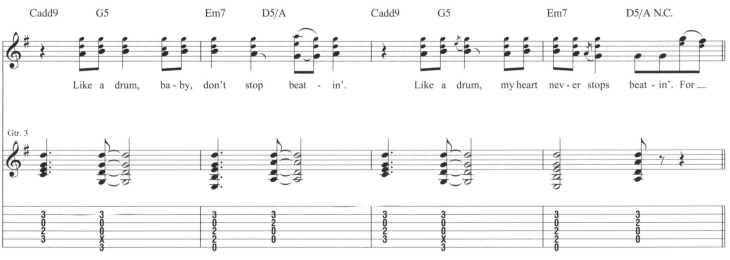

Like a drum, ba - by, don't stop beat - in'. Like a drum, my heart nev - er stops beat - in'. For __

Chorus

Bkgd. Voc.: w/ Voc. Fig. 1
Gtr. 2: w/ Rhy. Fig. 1 (8 times)
Gtr. 3 tacet

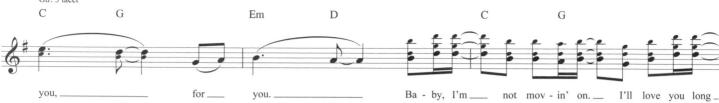

you, _____ for __ you. _____ Ba - by, I'm ___ not mov - in' on. __ I'll love you long _

Bkgd. Voc.: w/ Voc. Fig. 1

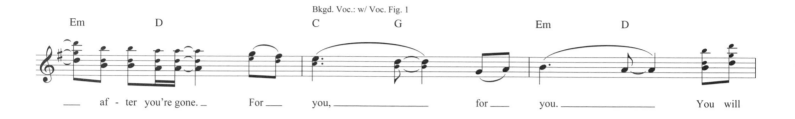

__ af - ter you're gone. _ For __ you, _____ for __ you. _____ You will

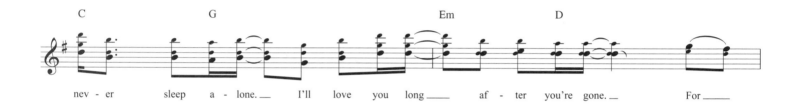

nev - er sleep a - lone. _ I'll love you long ___ af - ter you're gone. _ For ____

Bkgd. Voc.: w/ Voc. Fig. 1

you, _____ for __ you. _____ Ba - by, I'm ___ not mov - in' on. __ I'll love you long _

Bkgd. Voc.: w/ Voc. Fig. 1

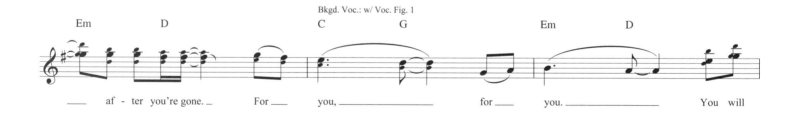

__ af - ter you're gone. _ For __ you, _____ for __ you. ____ You will

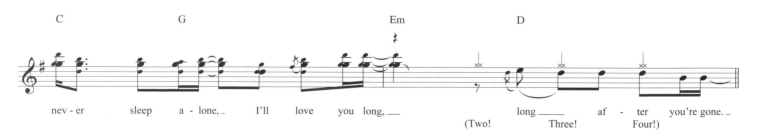

nev - er sleep a - lone, _ I'll love you long, __ long ___ af - ter you're gone. _
(Two! Three! Four!)

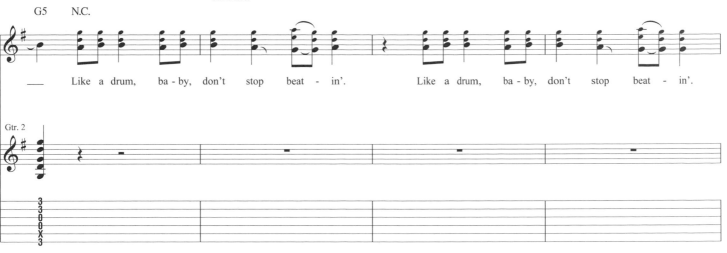

Like a drum, ba - by, don't stop beat - in'. Like a drum, ba - by, don't stop beat - in'.

Like a drum, ba - by, don't stop beat - in'. Like a drum, my heart nev - er stops beat - in' for

Outro

you. And long af - ter you're gone, gone,

gone, I'll love you long af - ter you're gone, gone, gone.

rit. poco a poco

Helplessness Blues

Words and Music by Robin Pecknold

Gtrs. 1 & 2: Open D6 tuning, capo I
(low to high) D-A-D-F♯-B-D

Gtr. 5: Open C5 tuning, capo III
(low to high) C-G-C-G-C-C

Intro
Moderately fast ♩ = 136

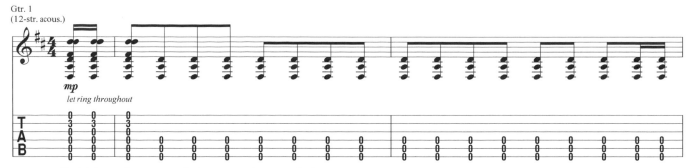

*Symbols in parentheses represent chord names respective to capoed guitar.
Symbols above reflect actual sounding chord. Capoed fret is "0" in tab.

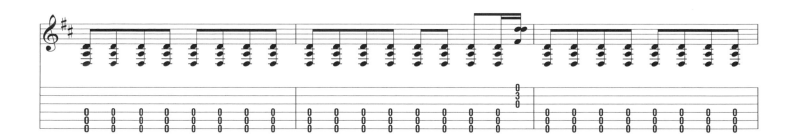

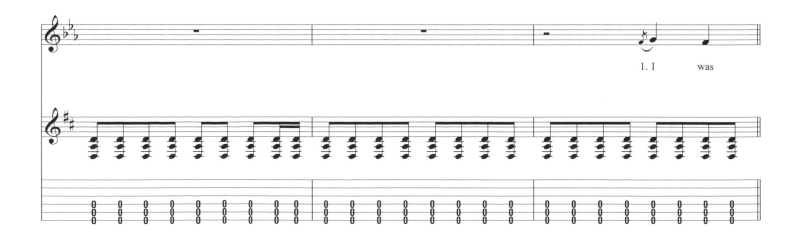

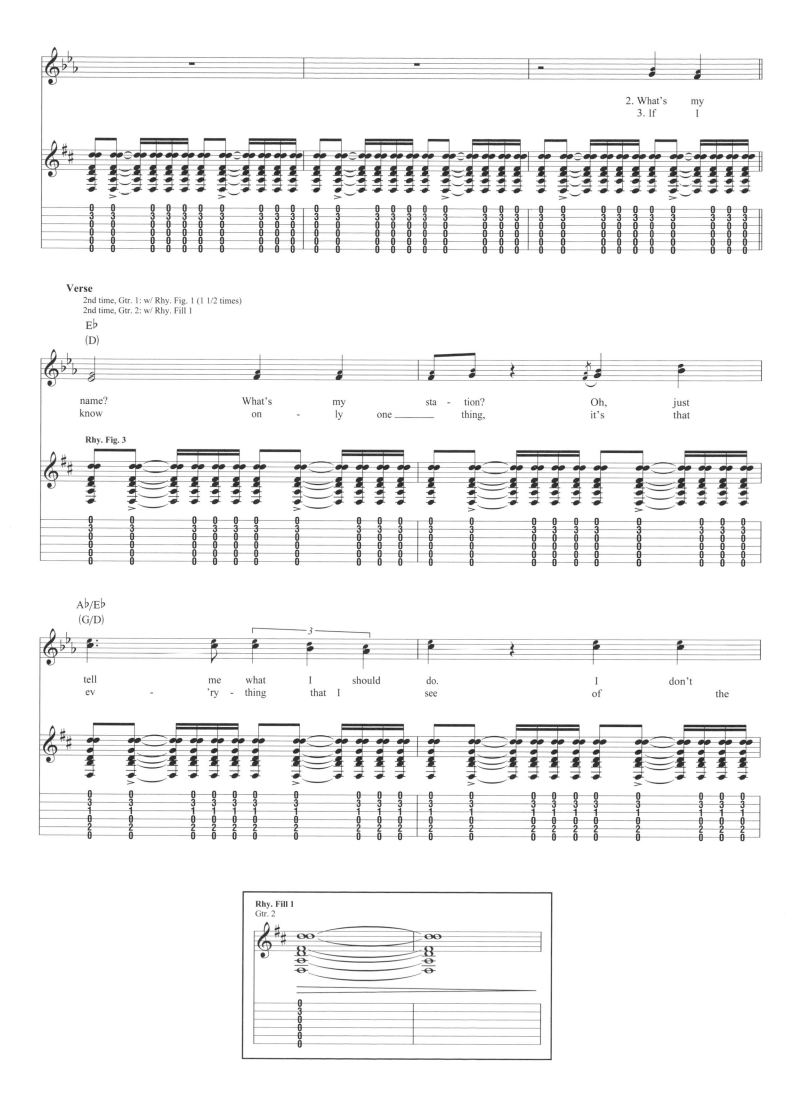

need to be kind to the ar - mies of night that would
world out - side is so in - con - ceiv - a - ble,

do such in - jus - tice to _____ you or bow
of - ten I bare - ly can speak. Yeah, I'm

End Rhy. Fig. 3

1st time, Gtrs. 1 & 2: w/ Rhy. Fig. 3

down and be grate - ful, and say, "Sure, take all that you see" to _____ the
tongue - tied and diz - zy, and I can't keep it to my - self. What

2nd time, Gtrs. 1 & 2: w/ Rhy. Fig. 3 (last 4 meas.)

men who move on - ly in dim - ly lit halls and de - ter - mine my fut - ure for _____ me. And I
good is it to sing help - less - ness blues? Why should I wait for an - y - one else? And I

Chorus
Gtrs. 1 & 2: w/ Rhy. Fig. 2

know, I _____ know you _____ will keep me on the shelf. I'll come back to you some - day soon _____

42

Outro

Ho Hey

Words and Music by Jeremy Fraites and Wesley Schultz

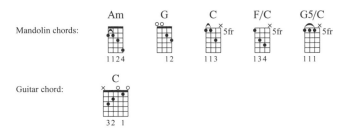

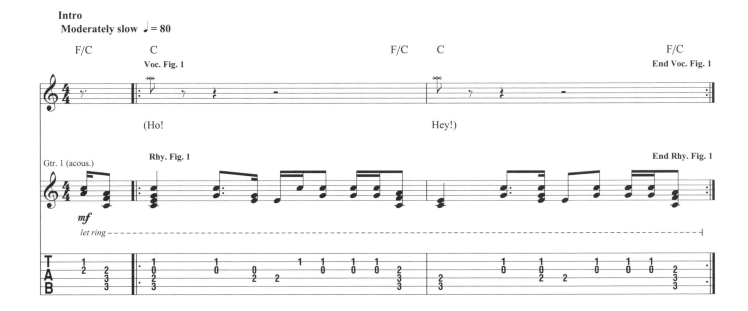

Intro
Moderately slow ♩ = 80

Verse

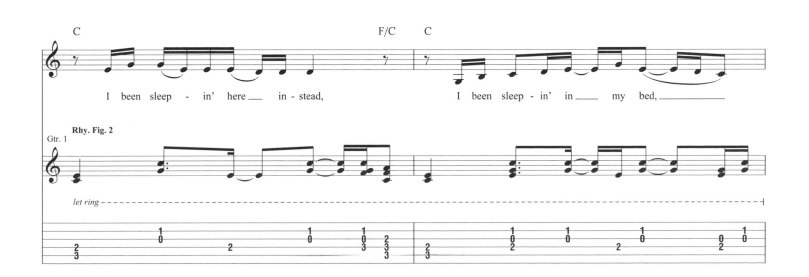

Chorus
Double-time feel

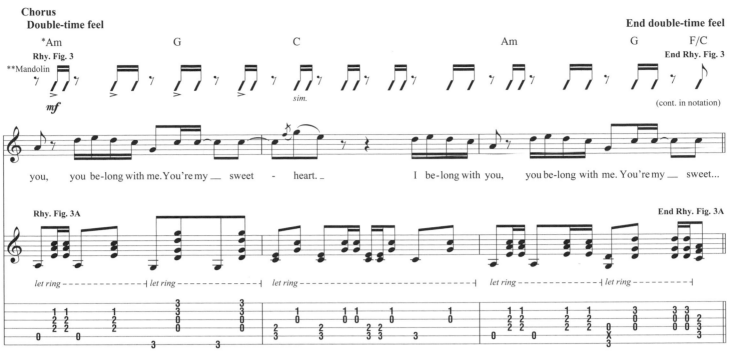

you,   you be-long with me. You're my __ sweet - heart. ___   I be-long with you,   you be-long with me. You're my __ sweet...

*See top of first page of song for chord diagrams pertaining to rhythm slashes.

**To play mandolin parts on guitar, capo 12th fret and tune highest four strings as follows: (low to high) G↓-D↓-A-E.

Interlude

Bkgd. Voc.: w/ Voc. Fig. 1 (4 times)
Gtr. 1: w/ Rhy. Fig. 1 (2 times)

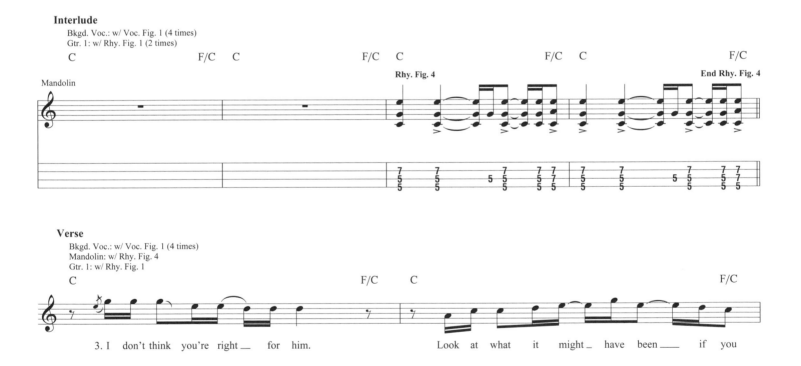

Verse

Bkgd. Voc.: w/ Voc. Fig. 1 (4 times)
Mandolin: w/ Rhy. Fig. 4
Gtr. 1: w/ Rhy. Fig. 1

3. I don't think you're right __ for him.   Look at what it might __ have been ___ if you

Gtr. 1: w/ Rhy. Fig. 2

took a bus to Chi - na-town.   I'd be stand-in' on __ Ca-nal ____   and Bow - er - y. ___

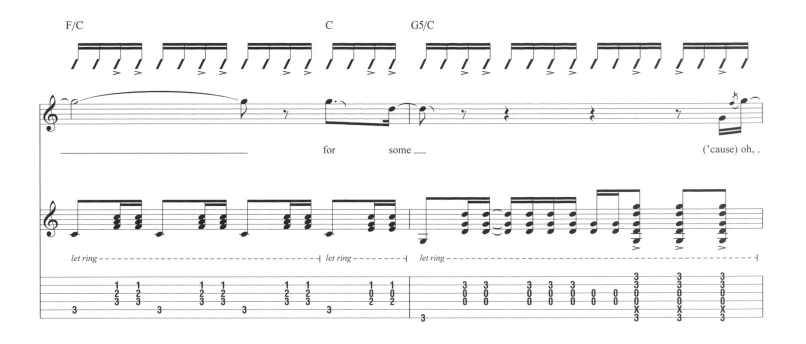

Mandolin & Gtr. 1: w/ Rhy. Figs. 5 & 5A

we're ___ bleed - in' out. ___ I be - long with

Chorus

Mandolin w/ Rhy. Fig. 3
Gtr. 1: w/ Rhy. Fig. 3A

End double-time feel

you, you be-long with me. You're my ___ sweet - heart. ___ I be-long with you, you be-long with me. You're my ___ sweet...

Outro

Gtr. 1: w/ Rhy. Fig. 1 (1 1/2 times)

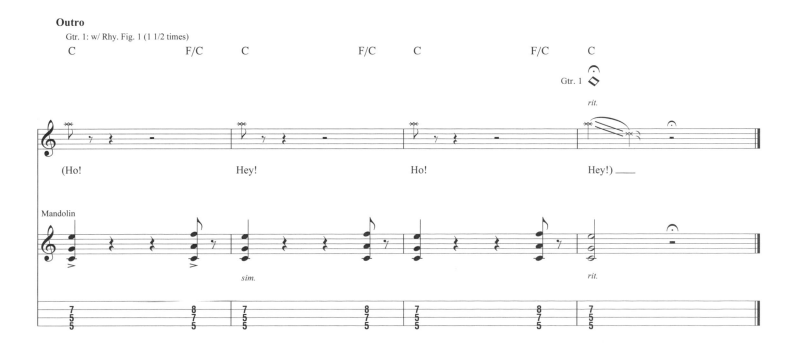

(Ho! Hey! Ho! Hey!) ___

Mandolin

from Edward Sharpe and the Magnetic Zeros - *Up from Below*

Home

Words and Music by Jade Castrinos and Alex Ebert

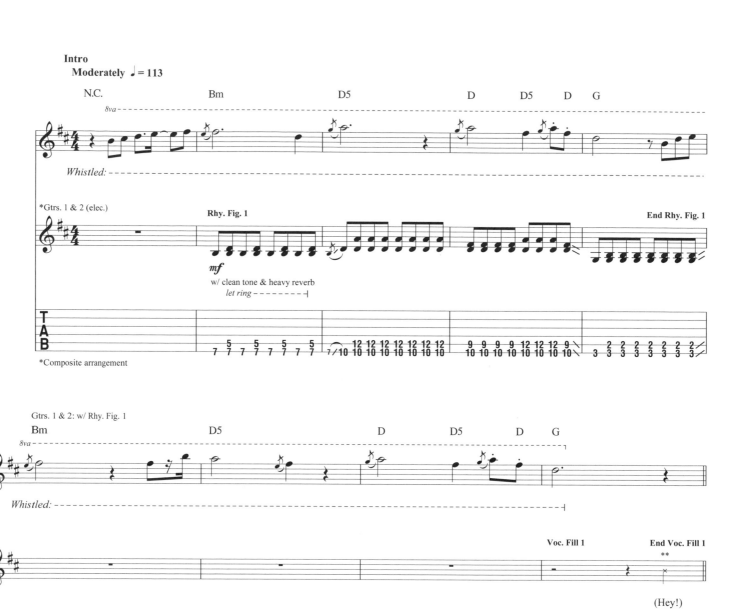

Verse

Female:
1. Al - a - bam - a, Ar - kan - sas, __ I do love my ma and pa, __ not the way __ that I do __ love __ you. __

Male: Well,

ho - ly mo - ley, me, oh, my, ___ you're the ap - ple of my eye. __ Girl, I've nev - er loved one __ like you. __

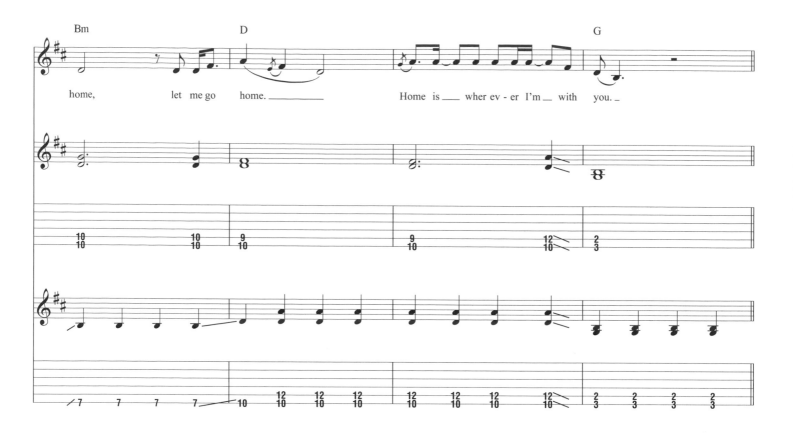

home,   let me go   home. _____   Home is ___ wher ev - er I'm ___ with   you. _

Interlude

(Hey!)

Gtr. 3

Gtr. 4

*Gtrs. 1, 2 & 5

let ring - - - - - - - - - - - - - - - - | *let ring* - - | *let ring* - - - - - - - - - - - | *let ring* - - - - - - - - - - - - - - - - |

*Gtr. 5 (acous.), played **mf**.
Composite arrangement

*Male - full size
Female - cue sise

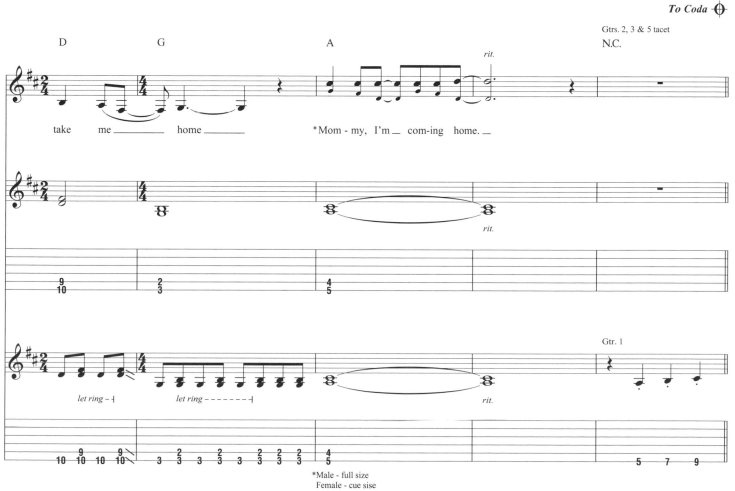

Interlude
A tempo

fol-lowed you in-to the park, _ through the jun-gle, through the dark. _ Girl, I've nev-er loved one _ like _ you. _

Female:
Moats and boats and wa-ter - falls, ____ al - ley - ways and pay-phone calls. _ I've been ev - 'ry - where _ with

Male: Yes.

you. _ ...we'll die, ___ ...sum-mer night, ___

That's true, heh. Laugh un - til we think we'll die, bare - foot on a sum - mer night, ____

*Female - full size
Male - cue size

D.S. al Coda

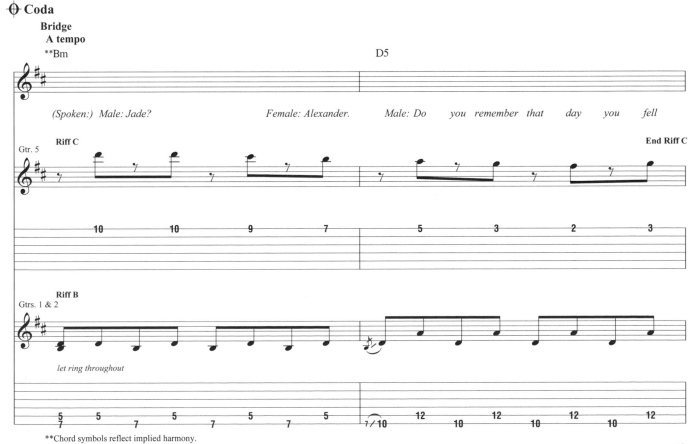

Coda

Bridge
A tempo

**Chord symbols reflect implied harmony.

Gtr. 5: w/ Riff C (7 times)

D   D5   D   G

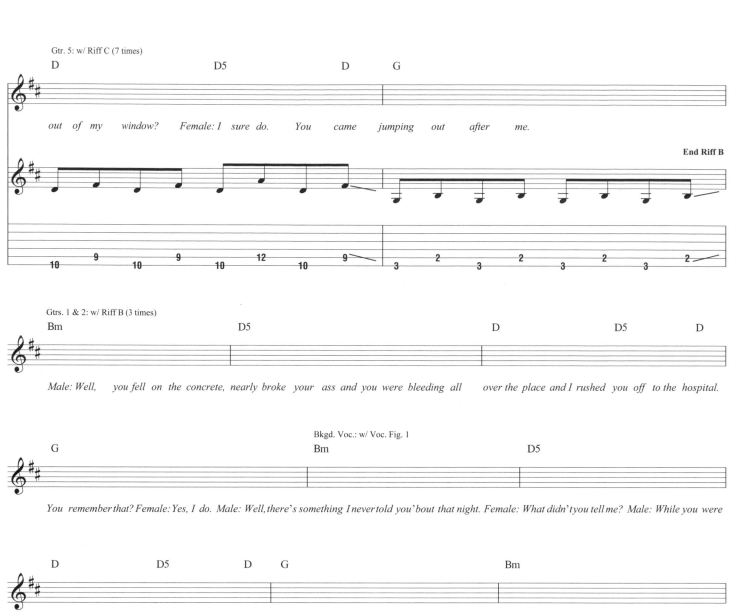

out of my window? *Female: I sure do.* You came jumping out after me.

End Riff B

Gtrs. 1 & 2: w/ Riff B (3 times)

Bm   D5   D   D5   D

Male: Well, you fell on the concrete, nearly broke your ass and you were bleeding all over the place and I rushed you off to the hospital.

Bkgd. Voc.: w/ Voc. Fig. 1

G   Bm   D5

You remember that? *Female: Yes, I do. Male: Well, there's something I never told you 'bout that night. Female: What didn't you tell me? Male: While you were*

D   D5   D   G   Bm

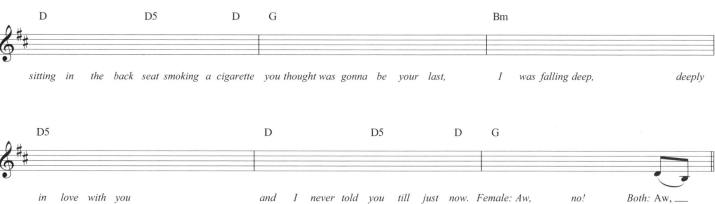

sitting in the back seat smoking a cigarette you thought was gonna be your last, I was falling deep, deeply

D5   D   D5   D   G

in love with you and I never told you till just now. *Female: Aw,* no! *Both: Aw,* __

Chorus

Bkgd. Voc.: w/ Voc. Fig. 1
Gtrs. 1 & 2: w/ Rhy. Fig. 1 (2 times)
Gtr. 3: w/ Rhy. Fig. 2 (2 times)
Gtr. 4: w/ Riff A (1 1/2 times)
Gtr. 5: w/ Riff C (4 times)

Bm   D

home, let me go home, home is __ when - ev - er I'm __ with

G   Bm   D

you. __ Aw, __ home, let me go home. __

Female: Home. __

from Milk Carton Kids - *The Ash & Clay*

Hope of a Lifetime

Words and Music by Kenneth Pattengale and Joseph Ryan

Gtr. 1: Capo VIII
Gtr. 2: Tune down 1 step, capo V:
(low to high) D-G-C-F-A-D

*Symbols in single parentheses represent chord names respective to capoed Gtr. 1. Symbols in double parentheses represent chord names respective to capoed Gtr. 2. Symbols above reflect actual sounding chords. Capoed fret is "0" in tab. Chord symbols reflect implied harmony.

**2nd string bumped with pull-off finger.

Verse

calm   wind   in   the   pine,   for the

fate   of   a   fear - some   trav - es - ty

seems   to have   for - got - ten me, __

seems   to have   for - got - ten me. _____   If   it

End Rhy. Fig. 2

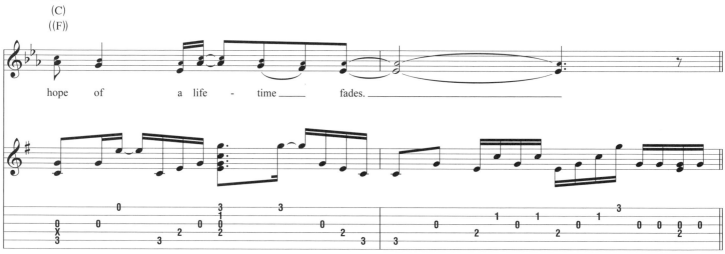

Interlude

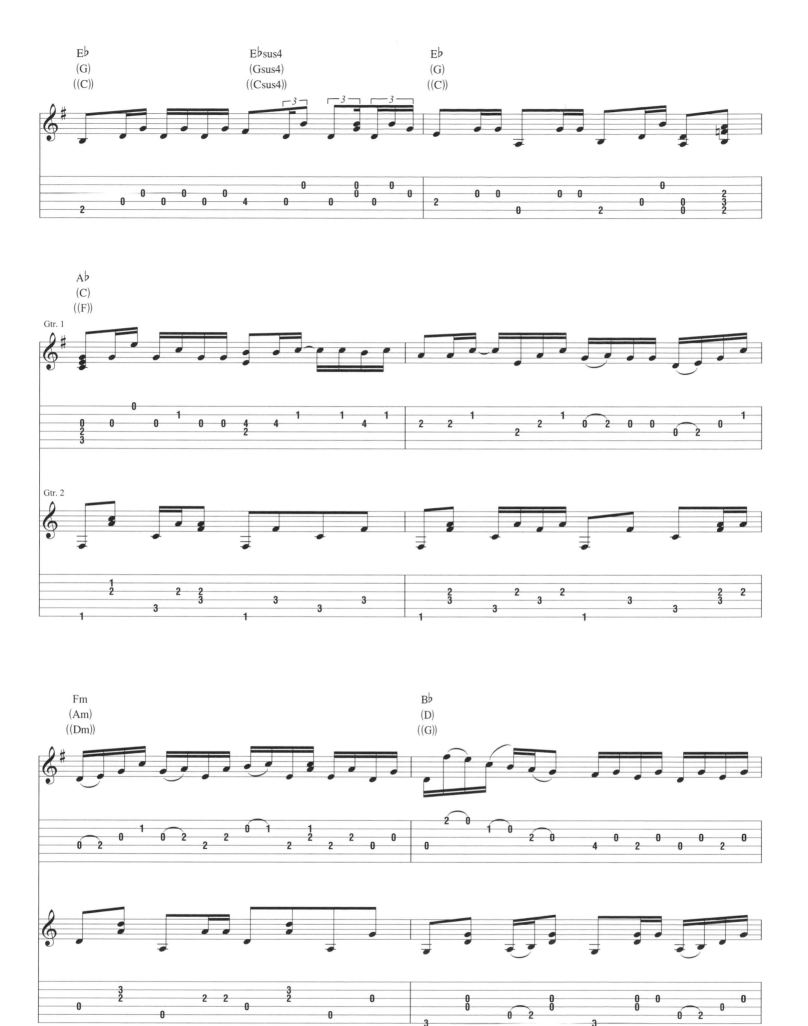

hold   a   prom - ise   in the   air. _____

That's   the way   they   used   to find __   their   own   way   home,

by   the   stars,   on   their own, _

by the   stars, _____   on   their   own. _____

Outro

Gtr. 2: w/ Rhy. Fig. 1 (1st 4 meas.)

*from Mumford & Sons - *Babel*

I Will Wait

Words and Music by Mumford & Sons

Open D tuning, down 1/2 step:
(low to high) D♭-A♭-D♭-F-A♭-D♭

Intro

Moderately fast ♩ = 132

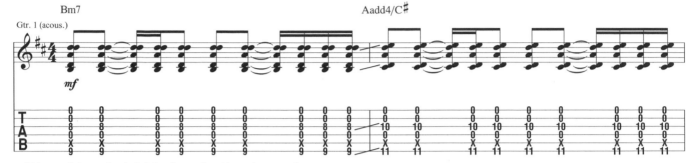

*This transcription matches the *Babel* studio recording. Live performances of
this song are in a different key, different tuning, and utilize different chord voicings.

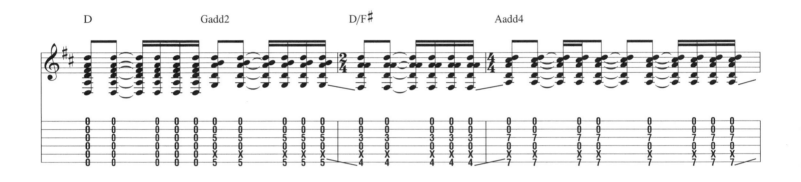

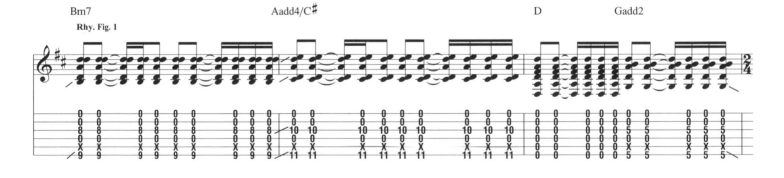

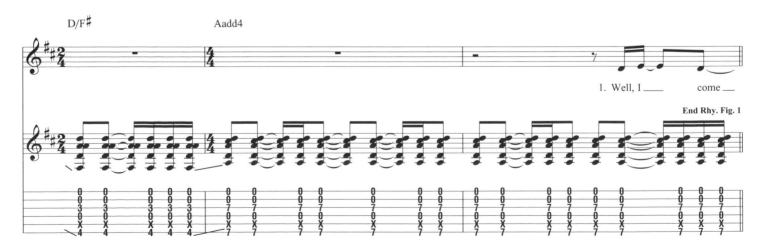

Verse

home _____ like a ____ stone, _____

*Slight P.M. where indicated throughout.

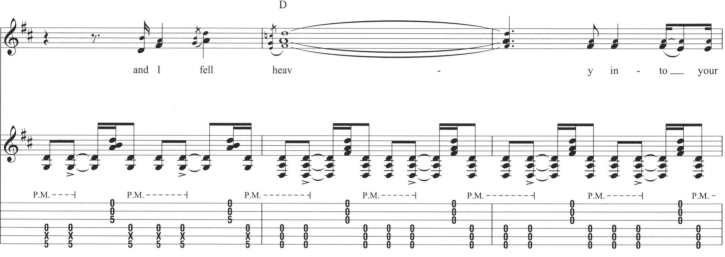

and I fell heav - y in - to ____ your

arms. These days ____

of dust ____ which we've ____ known ____ will blow a -

D   Aadd4

way _____ with this new _____ sun. _____   But

Pre-Chorus

Gtr. 1: w/ Rhy. Fig. 1 (2 times)

Bm7   Aadd4/C♯   D   Gadd2   D/F♯

I'll _____ kneel _____ down, wait _____ for

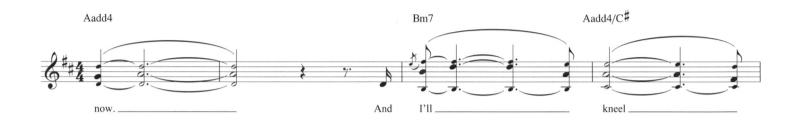

Aadd4   Bm7   Aadd4/C♯

now. _____ And I'll _____ kneel _____

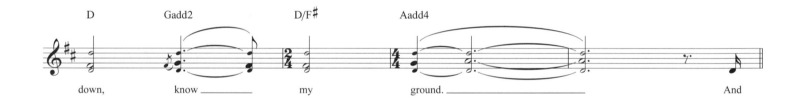

D   Gadd2   D/F♯   Aadd4

down, know _____ my ground. _____   And

Chorus

D   F♯m♭6   Aadd4

I will __ wait, I will wait for you. _____   And

Gtr. 1   **Rhy. Fig. 3**   **End Rhy. Fig. 3**

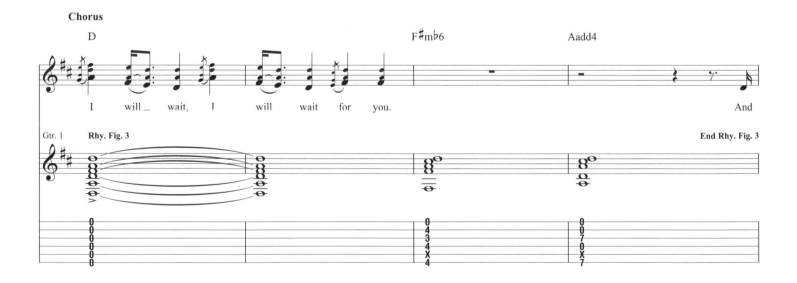

Gtr. 1: w/ Rhy. Fig. 3

D   F♯m♭6   Aadd4

I will __ wait, I will __ wait for you.

Interlude

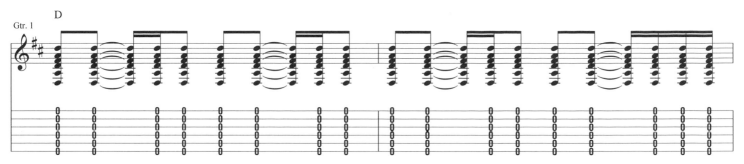

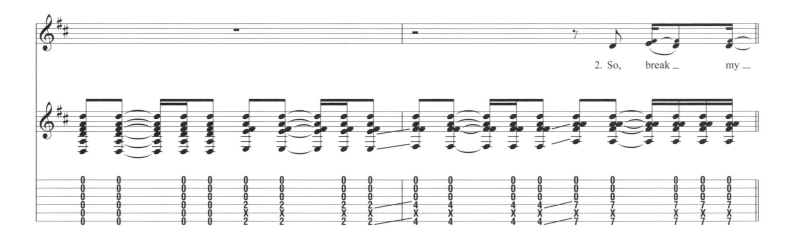

2. So, break _ my _

Verse

Gtr. 1: w/ Rhy. Fig. 2

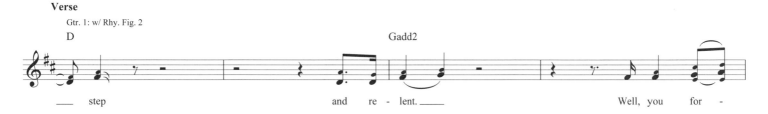

_ step and re - lent. _ Well, you for -

gave _____ and I won't _ for - get. Know what we've _

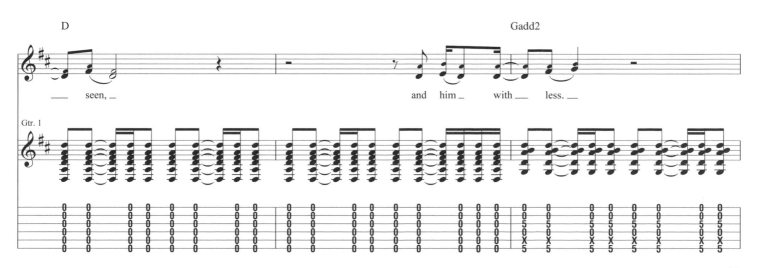

_ seen, _ and him _ with _ less. _

Gtr. 1

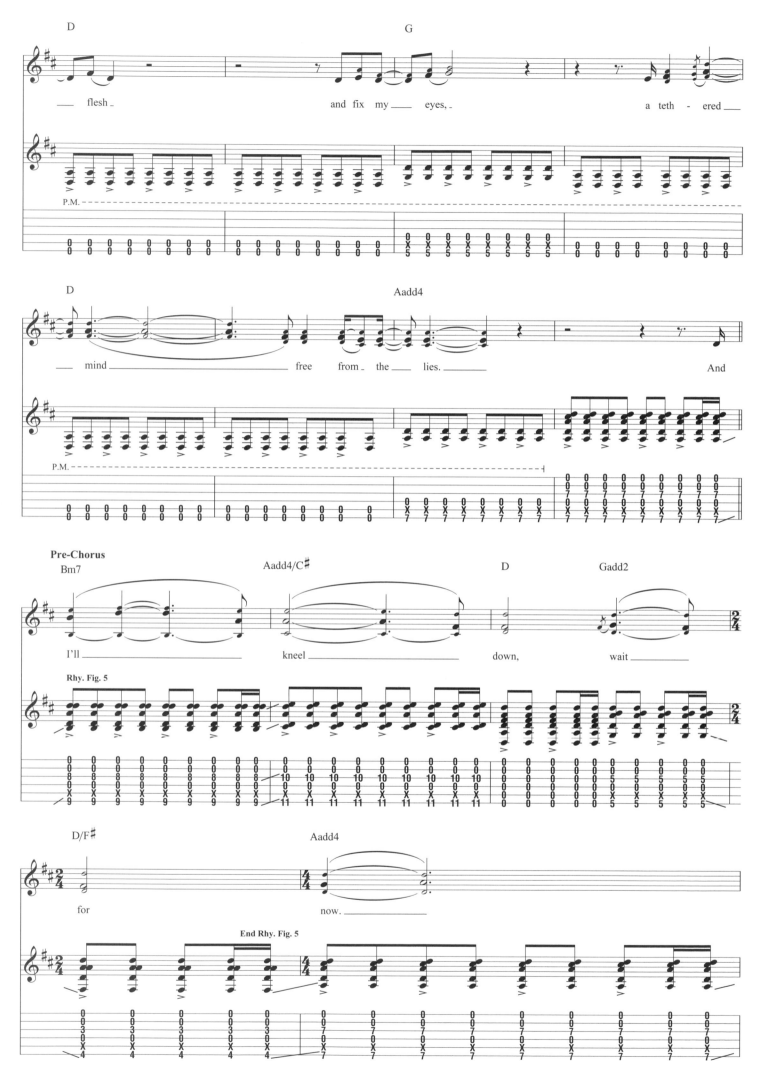

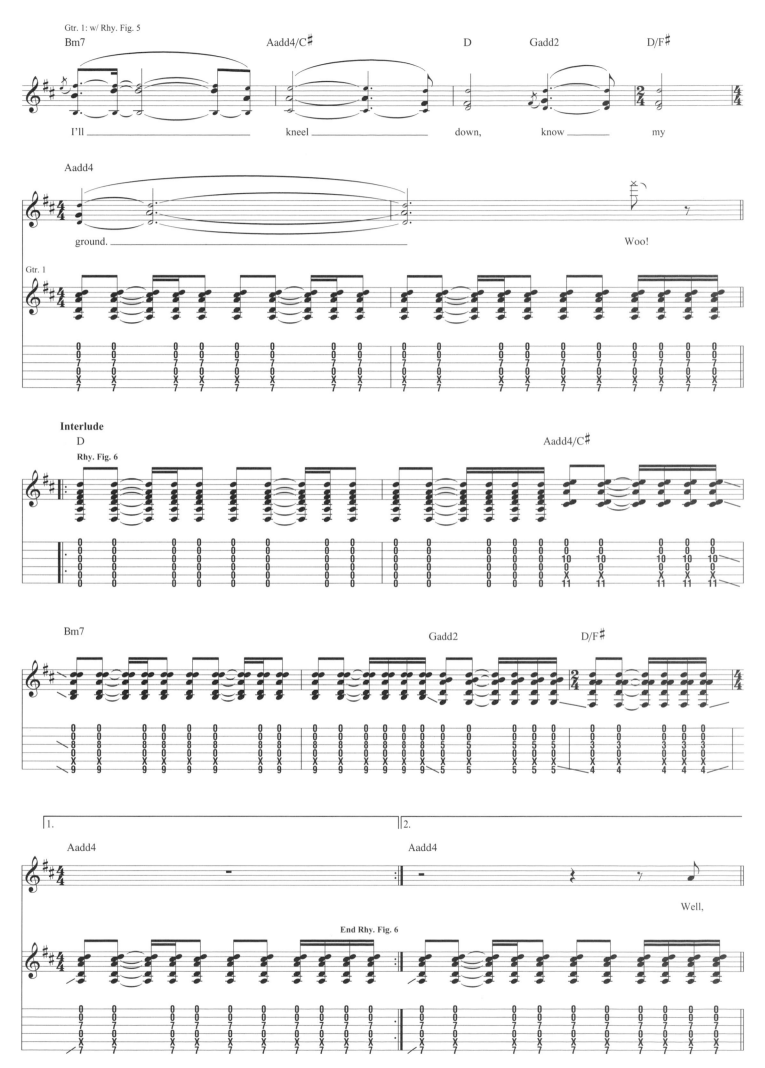

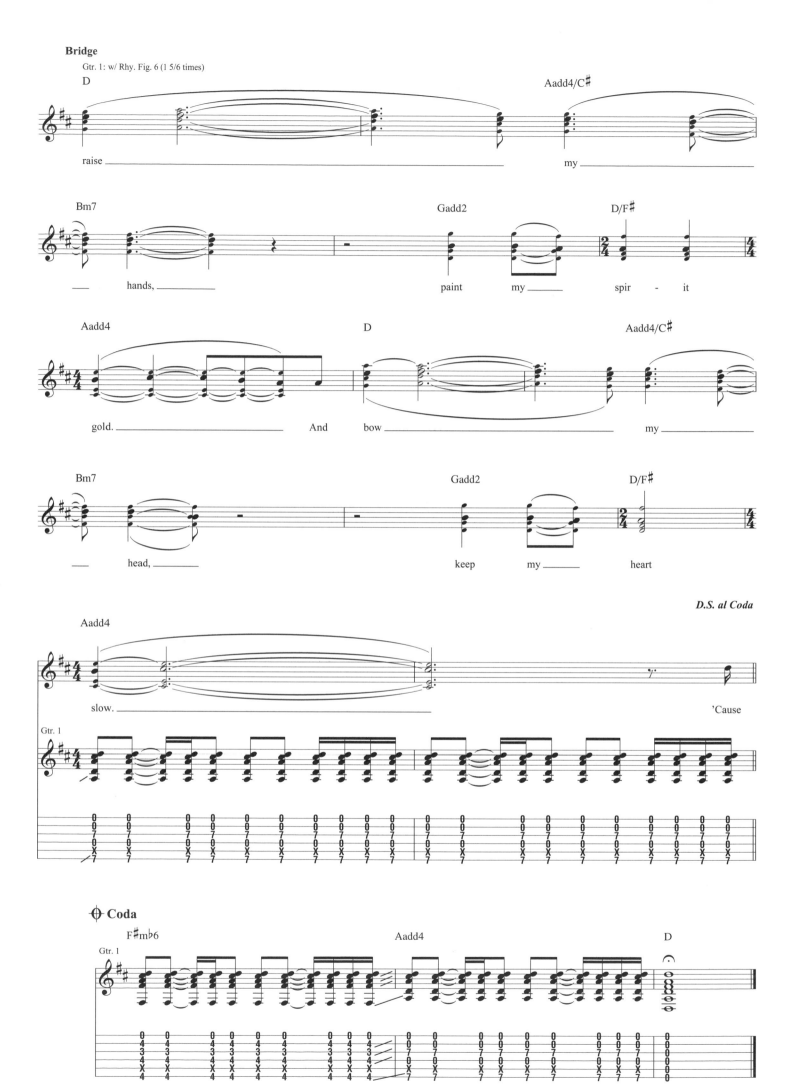

Little Lion Man

Words and Music by Mumford & Sons

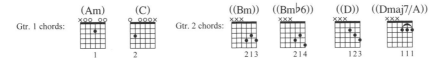

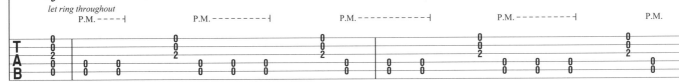

Gtr. 1: Open C6 tuning, capo V:
(low to high) C-A-C-G-C-E

Gtr. 2: Open G tuning, capo III:
(low to high) D-G-D-G-B-D

Intro
Moderately fast ♩ = 140

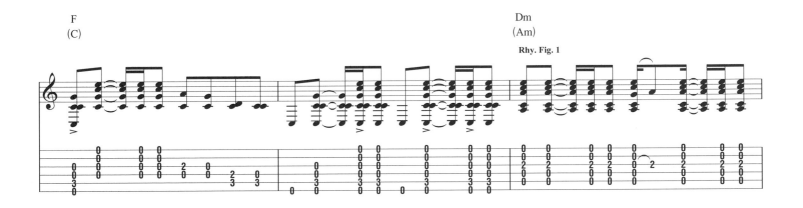

*Symbols in parentheses represent chord names respective to Gtr. 1. Symbols above represent actual sounding chords.
Capoed fret is "0" in tab. Chord symbols reflect overall harmony.

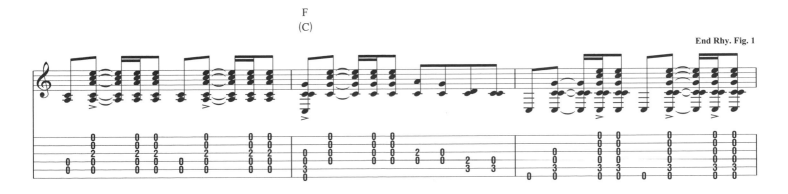

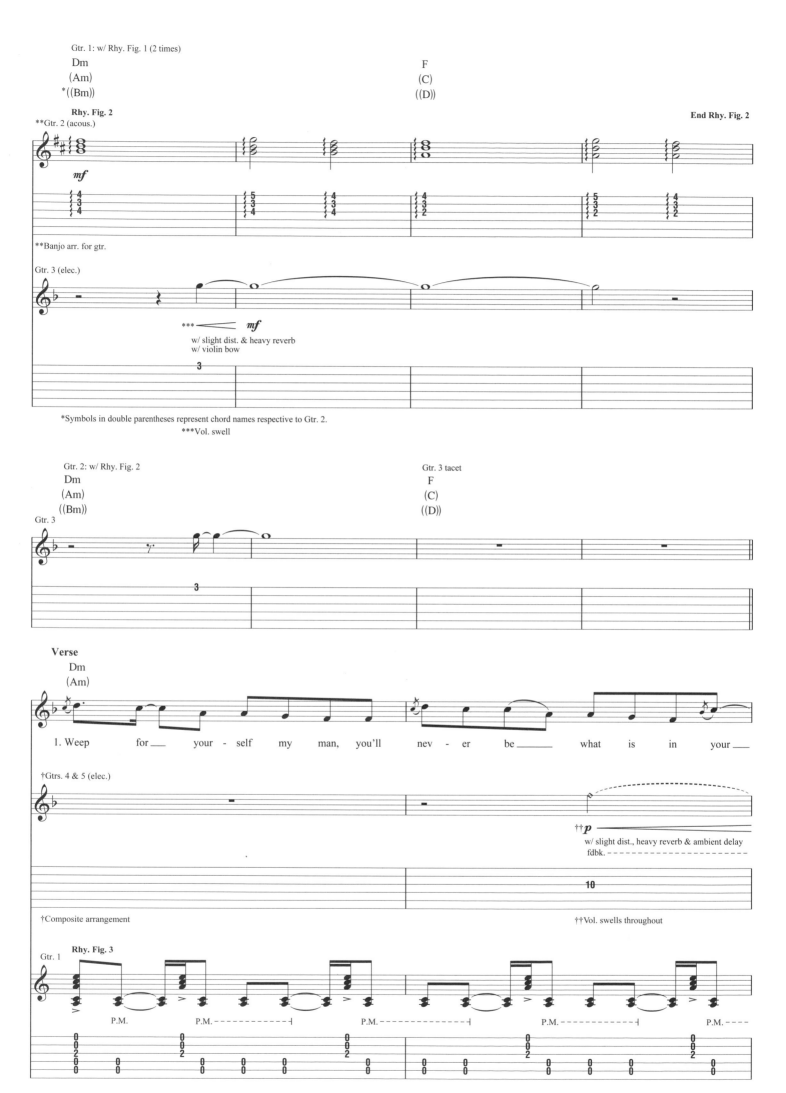

Verse

*See top of first page of song for chord diagrams pertaining to rhythm slashes.

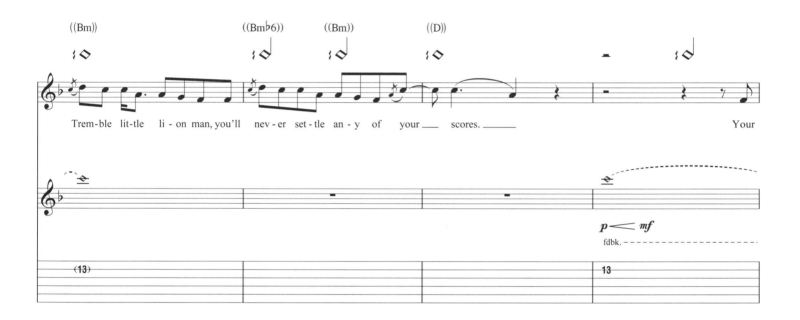

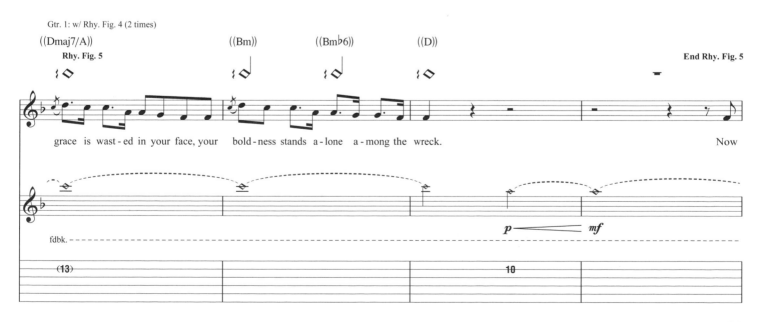

Bridge

from Of Monsters and Men - *My Head Is an Animal*

Little Talks

Words and Music by Of Monsters And Men

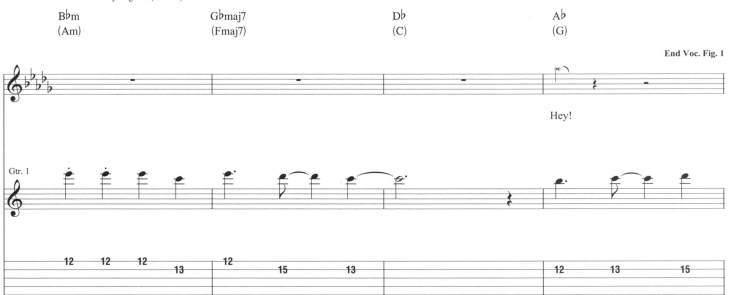

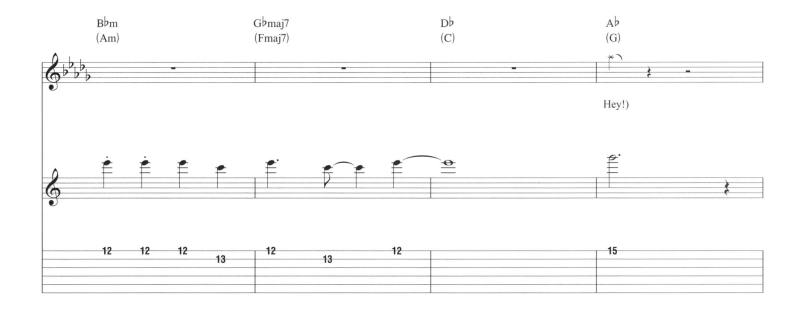

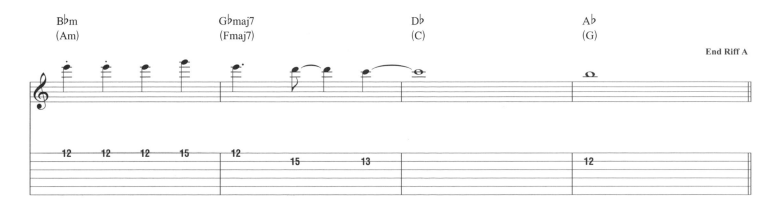

2nd time, Gtrs. 2, 3 & 4: w/ Rhy. Fig. 3 (6 times)   Gtrs. 1, 3, 4 & 5 tacet
2nd time, Gtr. 5: w/ Rhy. Fig. 3A (6 times)

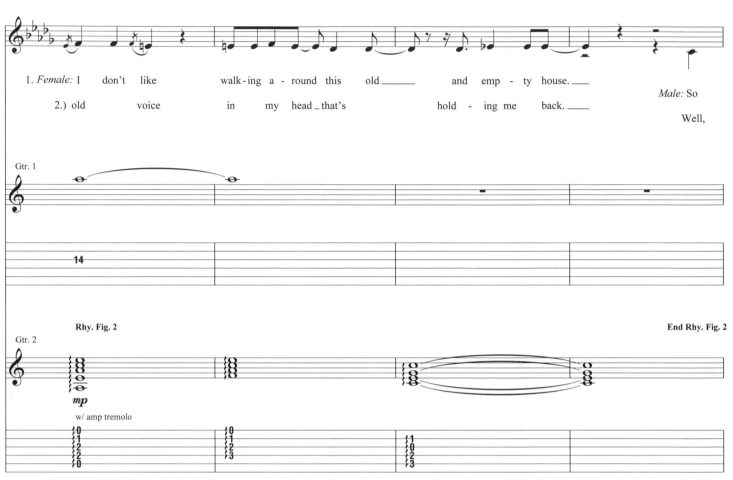

1. *Female:* I don't like walk-ing a-round this old ___ and emp-ty house. ___   *Male:* So

2.) old voice in my head that's hold-ing me back. ___   Well,

*See top of first page of song for chord diagrams pertaining to rhythm slashes.

Gtr. 2: w/ Rhy. Fig. 2 (3 times)

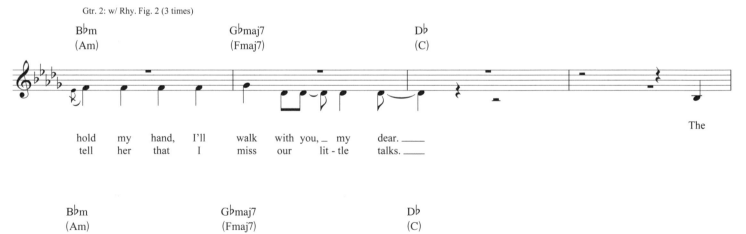

B♭m	G♭maj7	D♭
(Am)	(Fmaj7)	(C)

hold my hand, I'll walk with you, _ my dear. ___   The

tell her that I miss our lit-tle talks. ___

B♭m	G♭maj7	D♭
(Am)	(Fmaj7)	(C)

stairs creek as you sleep, _ it's keep-ing me a-wake. ___   It's the

Soon it will be o-ver ___ and bur-ied with our ___ past.   We

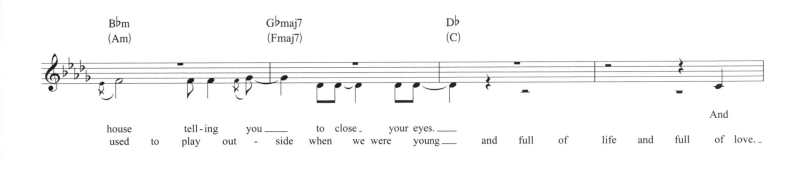

house tell-ing you_____ to close____ your eyes._____
used to play out - side when we were young____ and full of life and full of love.__

And

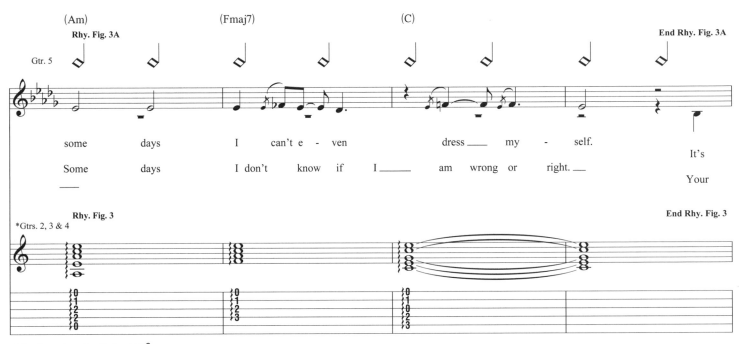

some days I can't e - ven dress____ my - self.
Some days I don't know if I_____ am wrong or right.__

It's
Your

*Gtrs. 2, 3 & 4

*Gtr. 2: amp tremolo off, played *mf*

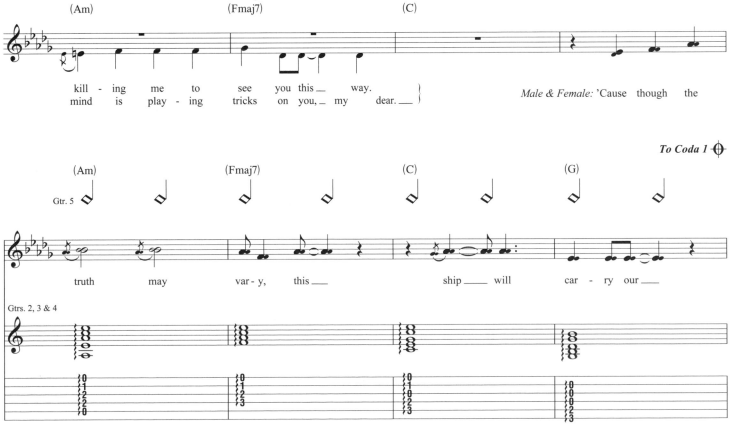

Gtrs. 2, 3 & 4: w/ Rhy. Fig. 3
Gtr. 5: w/ Rhy. Fig. 3A

kill - ing me to see you this__ way.
mind is play - ing tricks on you,_ my dear.__

Male & Female: 'Cause though the

To Coda 1

truth may var - y, this____ ship____ will car - ry our

Gtrs. 2, 3 & 4

Interlude

Gtr. 1: w/ Riff A
Gtrs. 2, 3 & 4: w/ Rhy. Fig. 1 (4 times)
Gtr. 5: w/ Rhy. Fig. 1A (4 times)

(*Yelled:* Hey!

Hey!

Hey!)

2. *Female:* There's   an

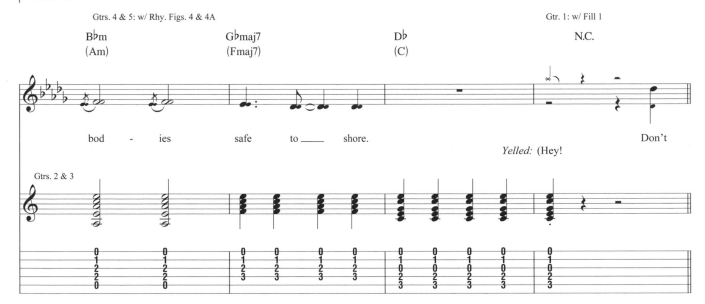

𝄋 𝄋 Chorus

1st & 2nd time, Bkgd. Voc.: w/ Voc. Fig. 1
1st time, Gtrs. 2, 3 & 4: w/ Rhy. Fig. 1 (4 times)
1st time, Gtr. 5: w/ Rhy. Fig. 1A (4 times)
2nd time, Gtrs. 2, 3 & 4: w/ Rhy. Fig. 1 (7 times)
2nd time, Gtr. 5: w/ Rhy. Fig. 1A (7 times)

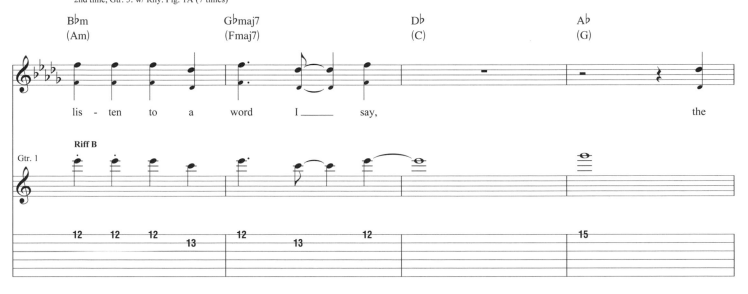

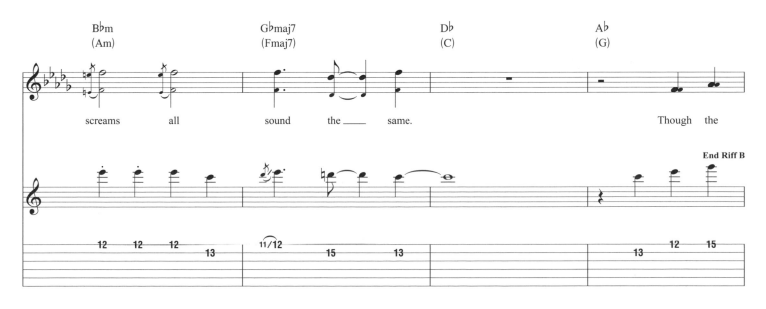

Interlude

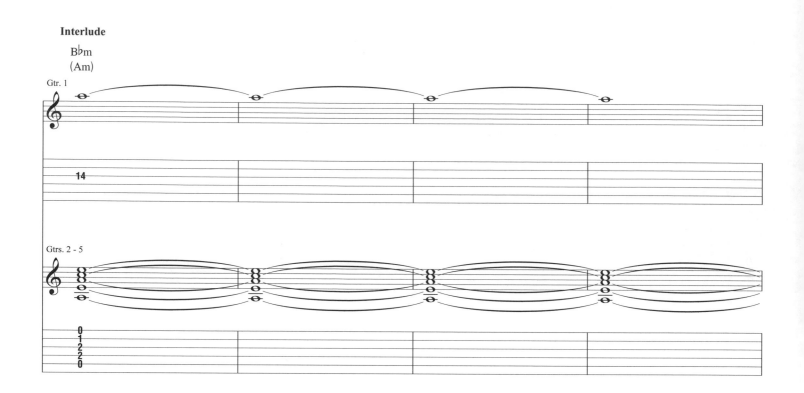

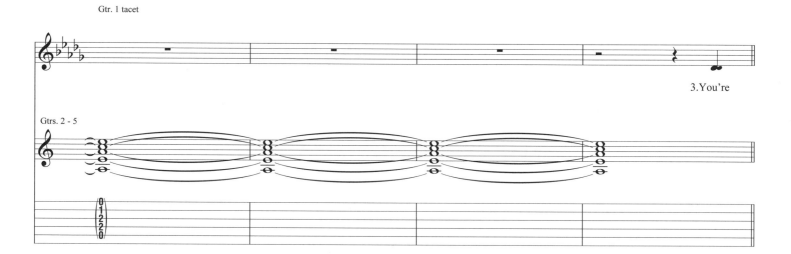

3.You're

Verse

gone, ___ gone, ___ gone a - way. ___ I watched you dis - ap - pear. ___

Coda 2

Outro-Chorus

truth   may   var - y,   this ___   ship ___ will   car - ry   our ___

bod - ies   safe   to ___   shore.   Though the

truth   may   var - y,   this ___   ship ___ will   car - ry   our ___

bod - ies   safe   to ___   shore.

from *The Carpenter*

Live and Die

Words and Music by Scott Avett, Seth Avett and Robert Crawford

Gtr. 1: Double drop D, capo IV
(low to high) D-A-D-G-B-D

Gtr. 2: Capo IV

*Banjo arr. for gtr.

**Symbols in parentheses represent chord names respective to capoed guitar.
Symbols above reflect actual sounding chords. Capoed fret is "0" in tab.
Chord symbols reflect implied harmony.

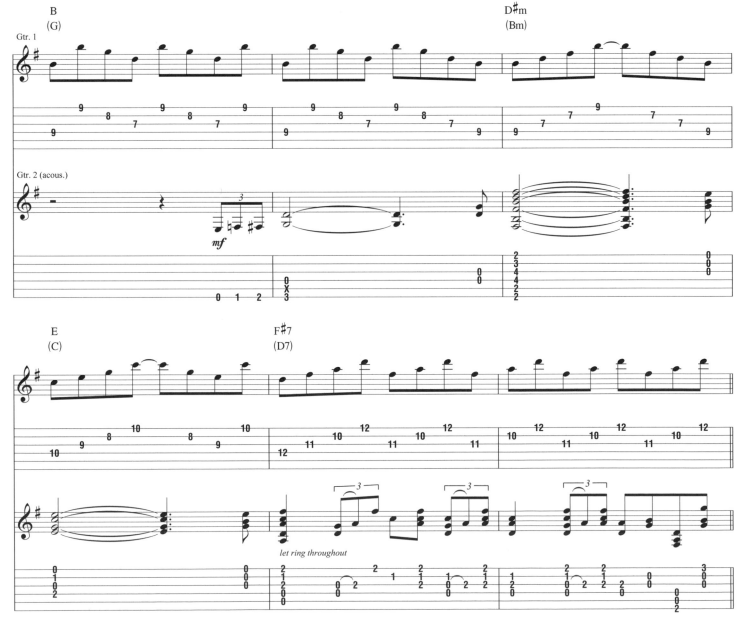

Verse

1. All it-'ll take is just one mo-ment and

you can say good-bye to how we had it planned.

Fear like a ha - bit, fun like a rab - bit, out _____ and a - way. ___

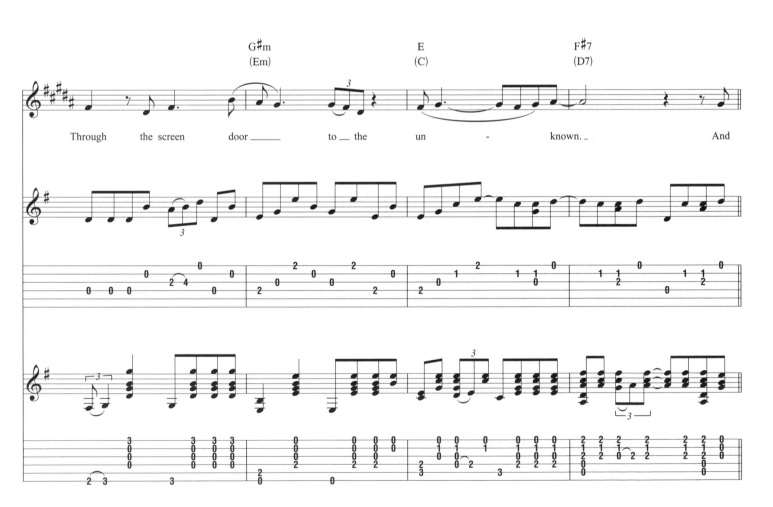

Through the screen door _____ to __ the un - known. ___ And

Pre-Chorus

Can ___ you ___ tell that I am a - live? ___ Let me prove ___

it. You and I, ___

Verse

2. Live like a phar-aoh, sing like a spar-row, an - - - y - way. __

E - ven if __ there is no __ land __ or love _____ in sight. __

119

Interlude

I ___ wan - na tempt you and more. ___

Can _____ you __ tell that I am a - live? _____ Let me prove _

Man on Fire

Words and Music by Alexander Ebert

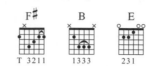

*Symbols in parentheses represent chord names respective to capoed guitar.
Symbols above reflect actual sounding chords. Capoed fret is "0" in tab.

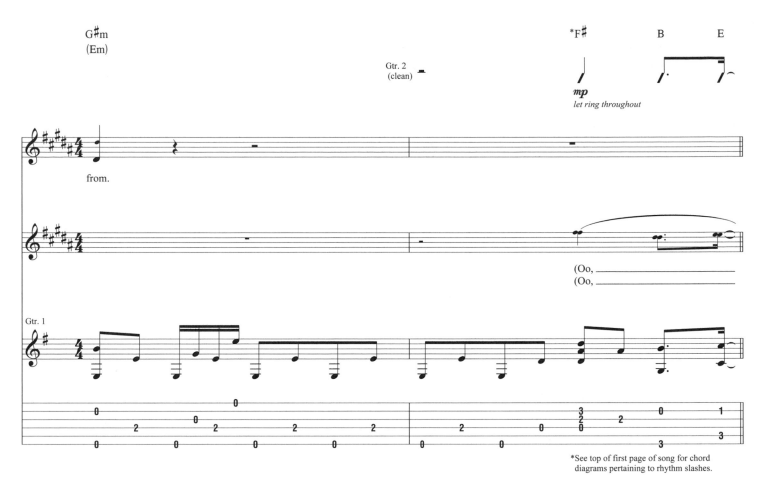

*See top of first page of song for chord diagrams pertaining to rhythm slashes.

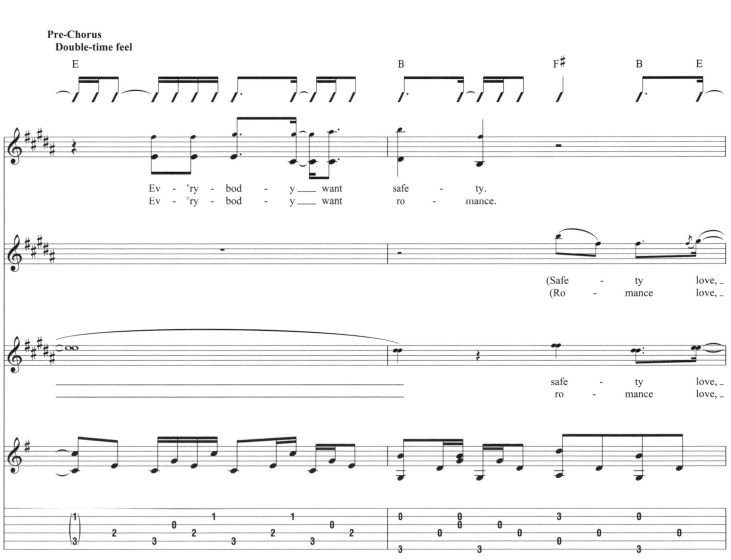

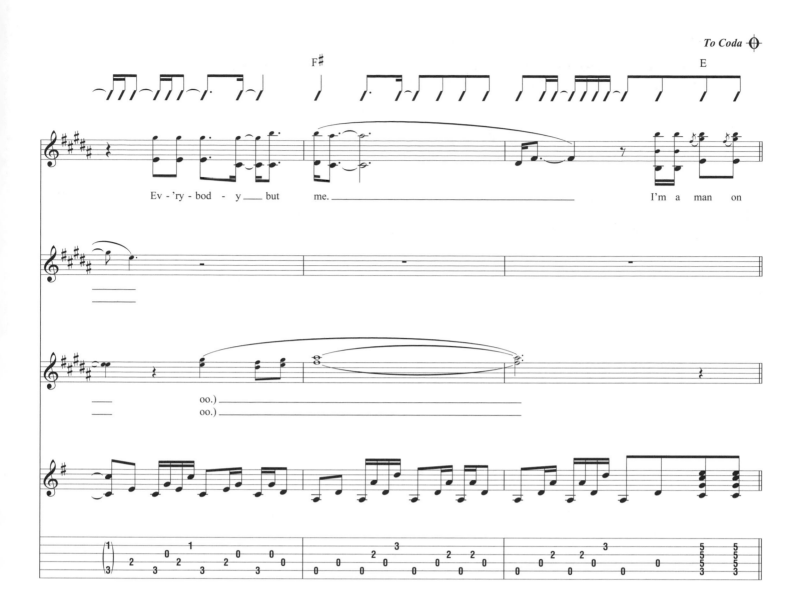

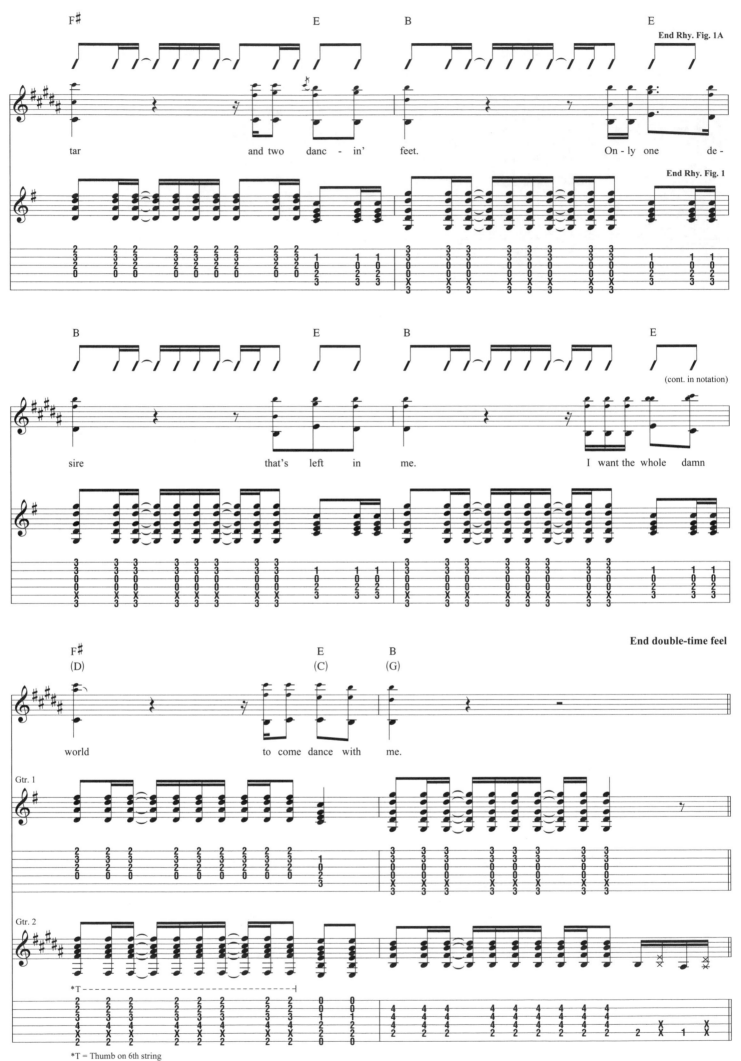

tar and two dancin' feet. Only one de-
sire that's left in me. I want the whole damn
world to come dance with me.

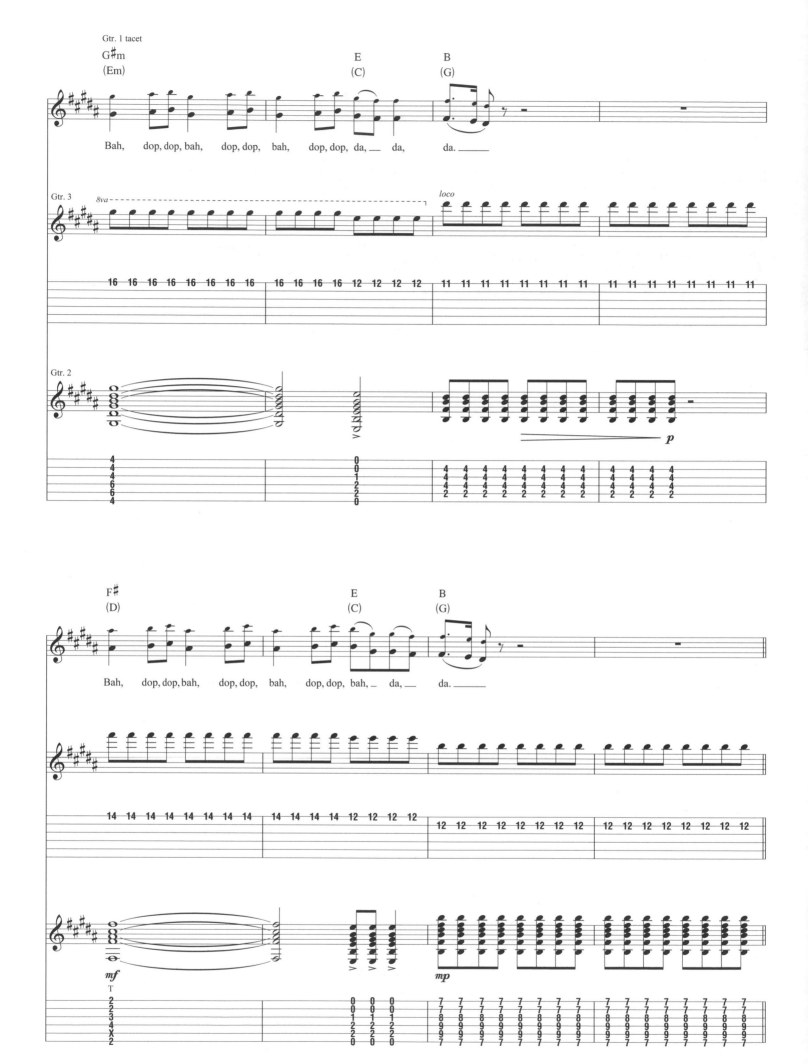

from Fleet Foxes - *Sun Giant*

Mykonos

Words and Music by Robin Pecknold

Gtr. 1: Capo II

*Symbols in parentheses represent chord names respective to capoed guitar.
Symbols above reflect actual sounding chord. Capoed fret is "0" in tab.
Chord symbols reflect overall harmony.

**Refers to both voices.

*T = Thumb on 6th string

149

to may-be dis-si-pate _____ shad-ows of _____ the mess you made. _____

Interlude

Bkgd. Voc.: w/ Voc. Figs. 1 & 1A (2 times)
Gtr. 2: w/ Rhy. Fig. 1 (2 times)

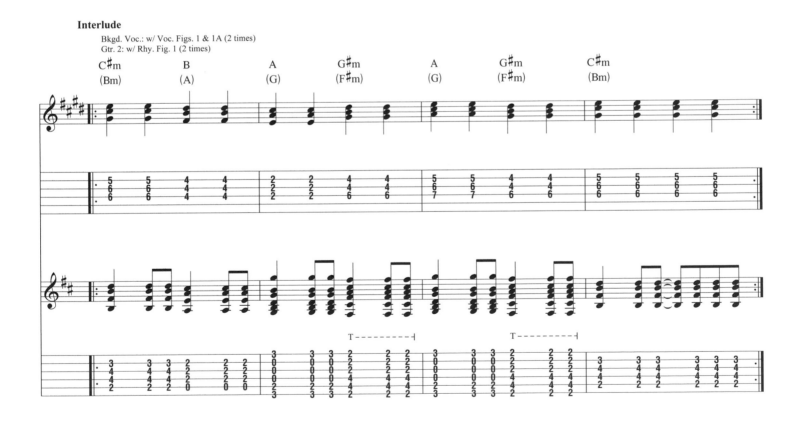

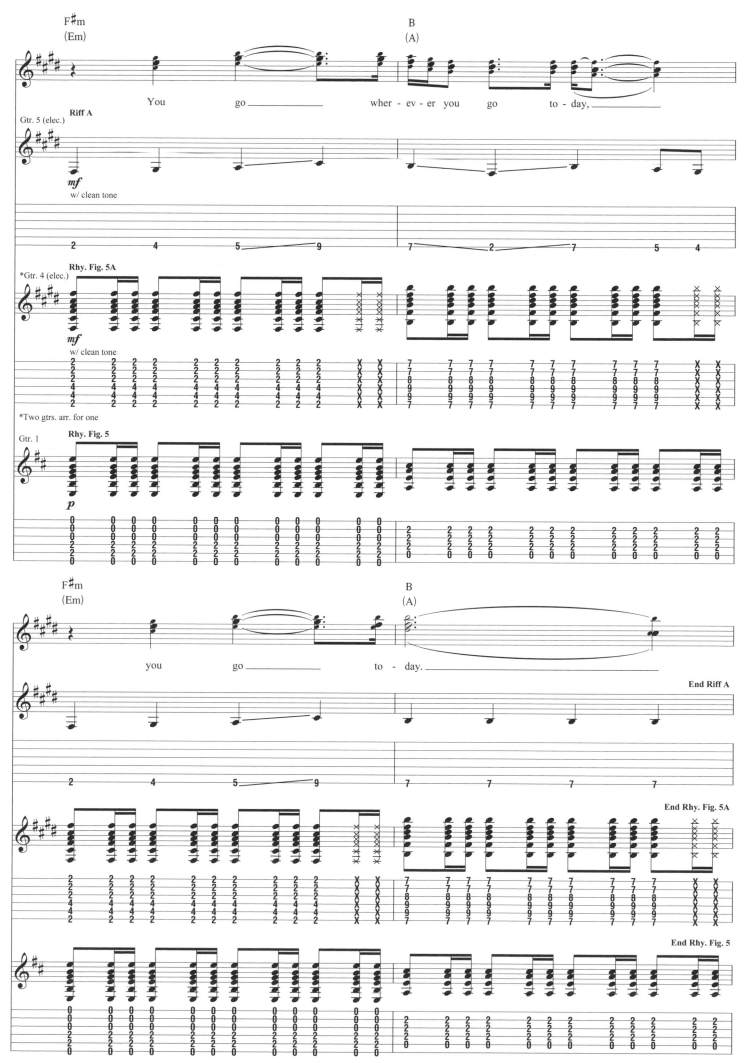

Gtrs. 1 & 4: w/ Rhy. Figs. 5 & 5A
Gtr. 5: w/ Riff A

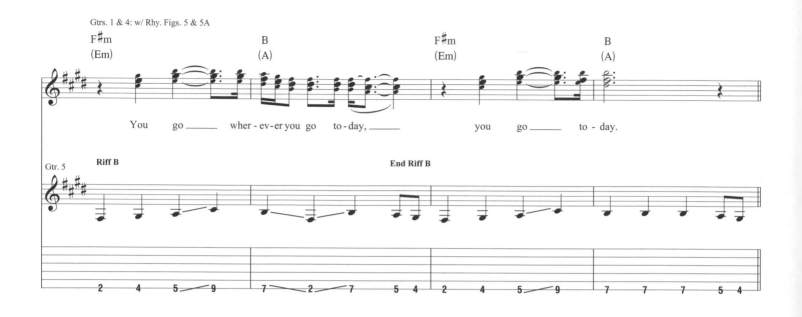

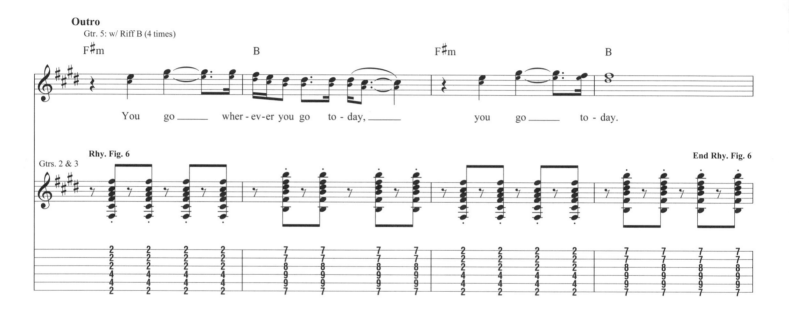

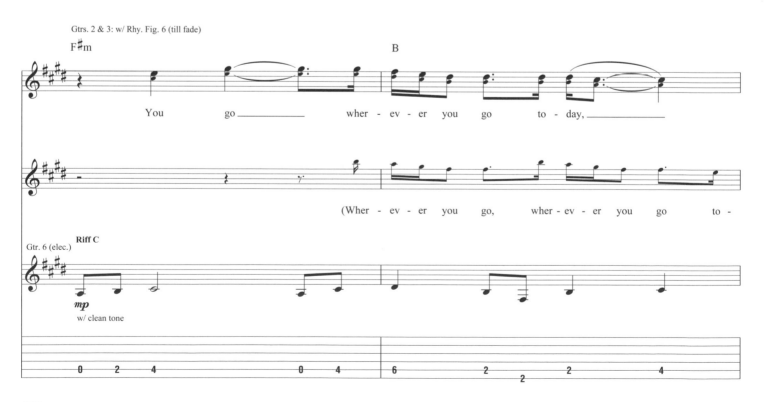

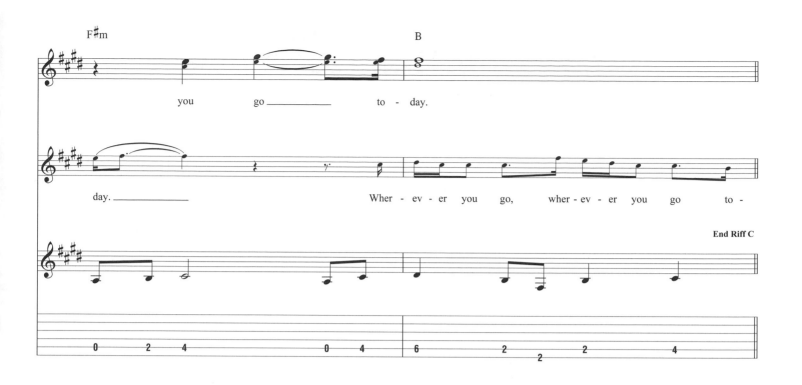

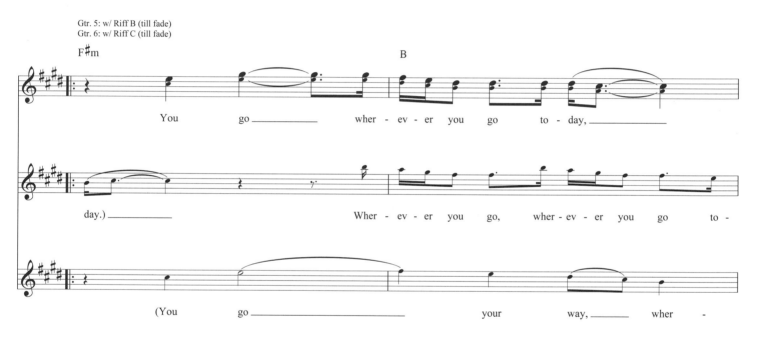

The One That Got Away

Words and Music by Joy Williams, John Paul White and Charlie Peacock

Gtrs. 1 & 2: Open D5 tuning:
(low to high) D-A-D-D-A-D

Gtr. 3: DADGAD tuning:
(low to high) D-A-D-G-A-D

Gtrs. 4 & 5: Open G tuning:
(low to high) D-G-D-G-B-D

Intro
Moderately slow ♩ = 73

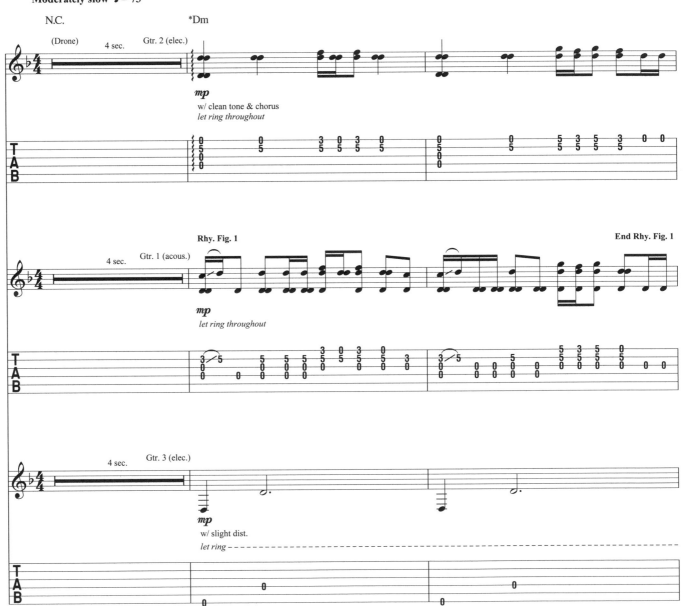

*Chord symbols reflect overall harmony.

Gtr. 1: w/ Rhy. Fig. 1

Female: 1. I

Gtr. 2

Gtr. 3

let ring

Verse

Gtr. 1: w/ Rhy. Fig. 1 (4 times)

Gtr. 2 tacet

Dm

nev - er meant _ to get us in _ this deep. _____

I

p

let ring

p

P.M.

*Bb

nev - er meant _ for this _ to mean a thing.

Well, I

Gtr. 3

P.M.

*Chord symbols reflect overall harmony.

159

Lyrics: wish ___ you were the one, ___ wish ___ you were the one ___ that ___ got a - way. ___

Interlude
Gtr. 1: w/ Rhy. Fig. 1
Gtr. 5 tacet

Dm

Verse

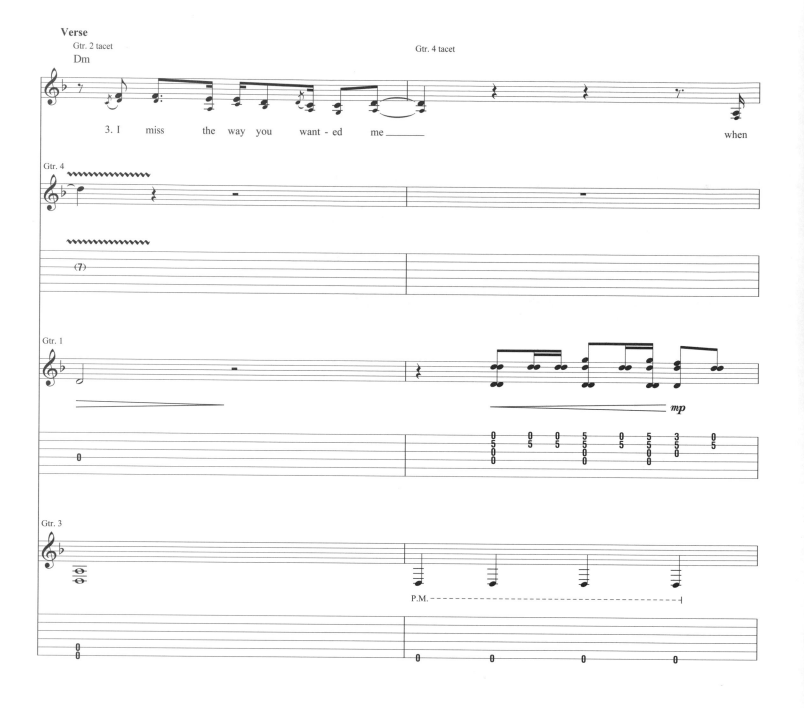

3. I miss the way you want-ed me _____ when

I was stay-in' just out of ____ your reach. ____

168

from The Civil Wars - *Barton Hollow*

Poison & Wine

Words and Music by John White, Joy Williams and Chris Lindsey

Gtr. 1: Capo II

Gtr. 2: Tune down 1/2 step:
(low to high) Eb-Ab-Db-Gb-Bb-Eb

*Symbols in parentheses represent chord names respective to capoed guitar.
Symbols above reflect actual sounding chords. Capoed fret is "0" in tab.

*Symbols in double parentheses represent chord names respective to detuned Gtr. 2 and do not reflect actual sounding chords.

Outro

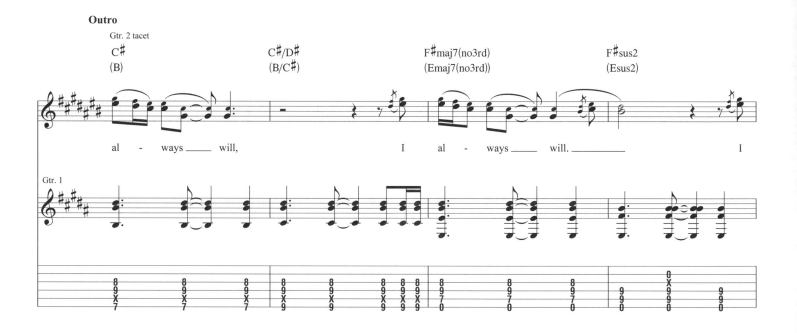

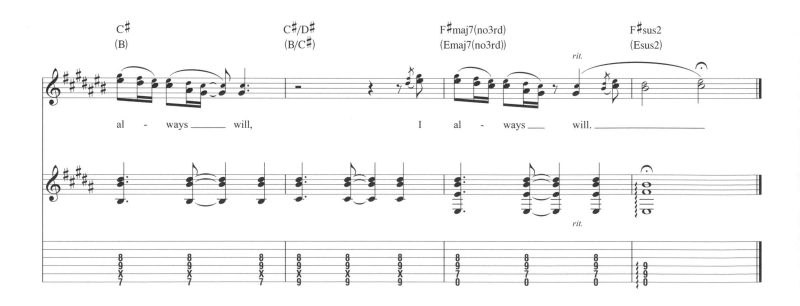

from Phillip Phillips

Raging Fire

Words and Music by Phillip Phillips, Gregg Wattenberg, Derek Fuhrmann and Todd Clark

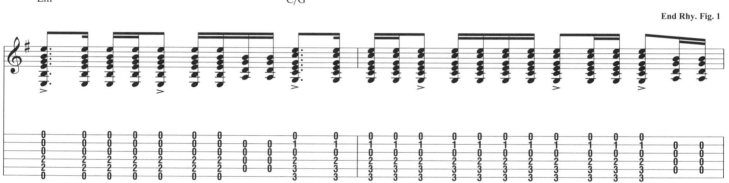

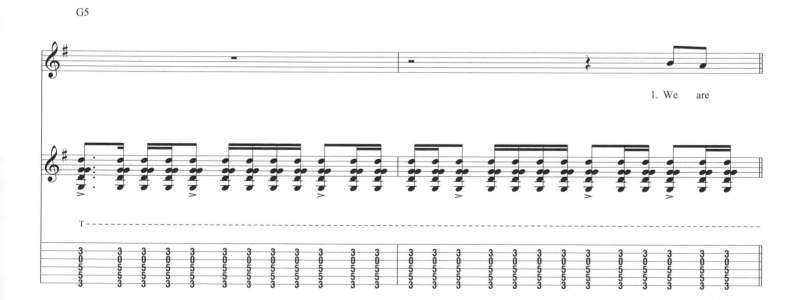

Interlude

Gtrs. 1 & 2: w/ Rhy. Fig. 1

G5   Em   C/G

fire? _____   2.You know
(Oh, _____ oh.) _____

Verse

Gtr. 1: w/ Rhy. Fig. 2 (1st 7 meas.)
Gtr. 2: w/ Riff A (1st 7 meas.)

G5

time will give ___ and time will ___ take. All the mem - 'ries ___ made ___ will wash a -

                    Em   C/G

- way. _____ E - ven though we've ___ changed _____ I'm ___ still here _____ with you. _

Gtr. 1: w/ Rhy. Fig. 2
Gtr. 2: w/ Riff A

G5

___ If you lis - ten close _____ you'll hear the sound

                                                          Em

of all ___ the ghosts ___ that bring ___ us down. _____ Hold on ___

D.S. al Coda

C/G   G5

___ to what makes you ___ feel. Don't let go, ___ it's what makes you ___ real. ___ If the

⊕ Coda   **Interlude**

Gtrs. 1 & 2: w/ Rhy. Fig. 1

G5   D5   G5

soul   in - to a rag - ing fire.

                                                        (Oh, _____

                    Em   C/G

                                                        Let the

_____ (Oh.) _____
(Oh.) _____
oh.)

177

178

from Bon Iver - *For Emma, Forever Ago*

Skinny Love

Words and Music by Justin Vernon

Open C tuning:
(low to high) C-G-E-G-C-C

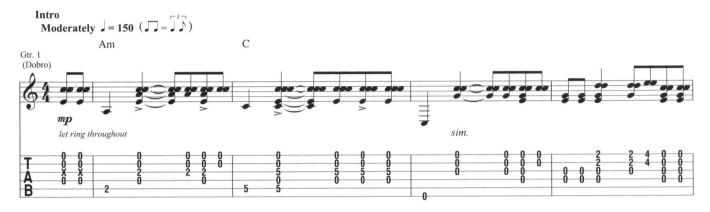

*Gtr. 2: Dobro
Composite arrangement

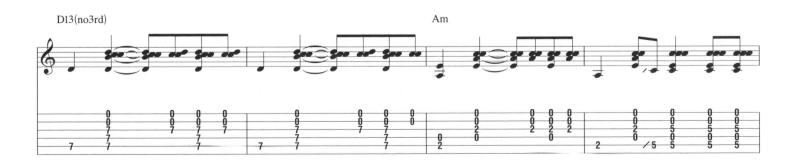

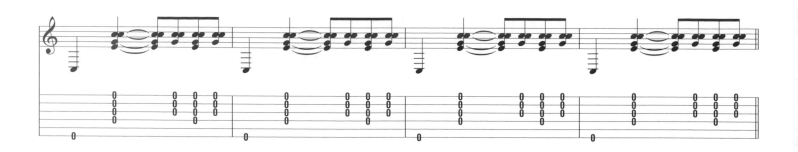

Verse

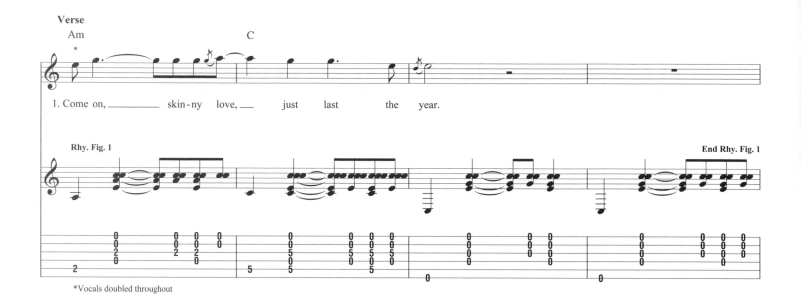

1. Come on, _____ skin-ny love, ___ just last the year.

*Vocals doubled throughout

Gtrs. 1 & 2: w/ Rhy. Fig. 1 (2 times)

Am   **C**

Pour a lit - tle salt, _____ we were nev - er here. _____ My, my, my, _

Am   **C**

___ my, my, my, ____ my, ___ my.   Star - in' at the

D13(no3rd)   **Am**

sink _____ of blood __ and crushed ve - neer.

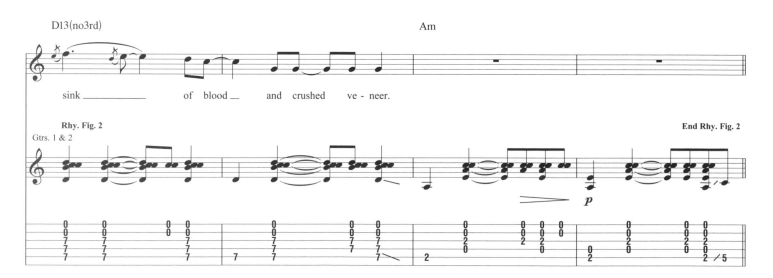

Gtrs. 1 & 2: w/ Rhy. Fig. 3 (2 3/4 times)

Cadd9/E   Gadd4/B   F/A

told you to ___ be bal - anced, and I told you to ___ be kind. ____ { And in the / And now

Cadd9/E   Gadd4/B   F/A

morn - in' I'll ___ be with ___ you, but it will be a dif - 'rent kind. _____ And I'll be
all ___ your love ___ is wast - ed. And then who the hell ___ was I? _____ And I'm

Cadd9/E   Gadd4/B

hold - in' all _____ the tick - ets, and you'll be own - ing all _____ the fines. ___
break - in' at _____ the britch - es, and at the end of all _____ your lines. ___

To Coda ⊕

F/A

Gtrs. 1 & 2

***2nd time, as before

*1st time, w/ random string plucks behind the bridge.

**1st time, as before

Verse

Am   C

3. Come on, _____ skin-ny love, ___ what hap - pened here?

Gtr. 1: w/ Rhy. Fig. 1 (2 times)
Gtr. 2: w/ Rhy. Fig. 1

Am   C

Suck - le on the hope ___ in light ___ bras - sieres. _____ My, my, my, -

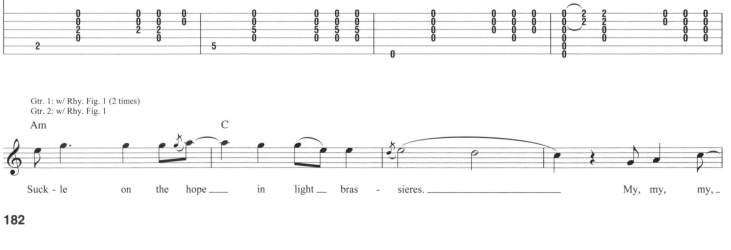

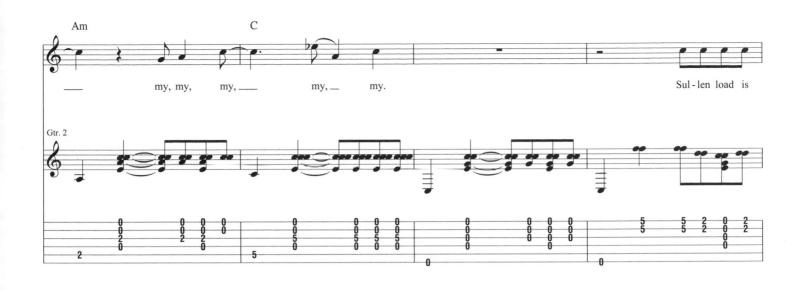

my, my, my, my, my.   Sul - len load is

full, _____ so slow on ___ the split. _____

And I've

⊕ Coda

Who will love you?   Who will fight? _

Who will fall _____ far be -

*As before

Outro

hind? _____

Oo. _____

Oo. _

**As before

from The Lumineers - *The Lumineers*

Stubborn Love

Words and Music by Jeremy Fraites and Wesley Schultz

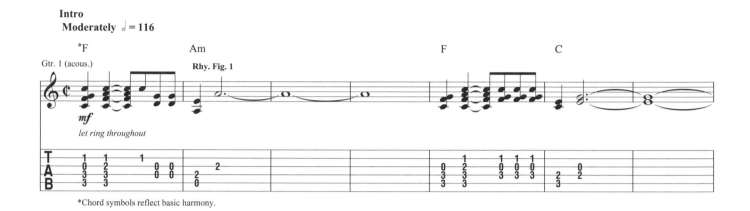

*Chord symbols reflect basic harmony.

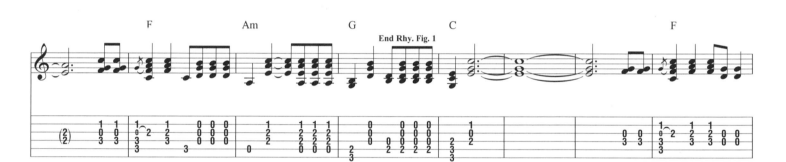

1. She'll lie and steal and

Verse

cheat ... and beg you from her knees.

Rhy. Fig. 2

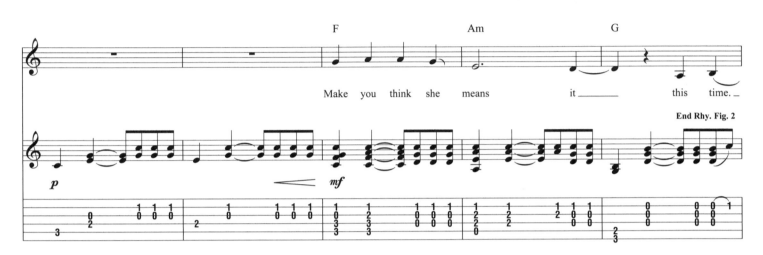

Make you think she means it _____ this time. ___

End Rhy. Fig. 2

Double-time feel

She'll tear a hole in

Gtr. 1: w/ Rhy. Fig. 2

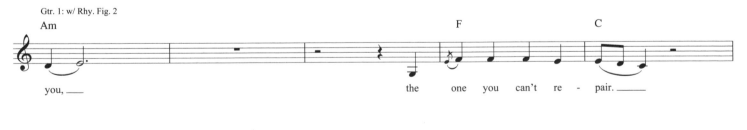

you, ___ the one you can't re - pair. ___

But I stilll love her, I don't real - ly care. ___

189

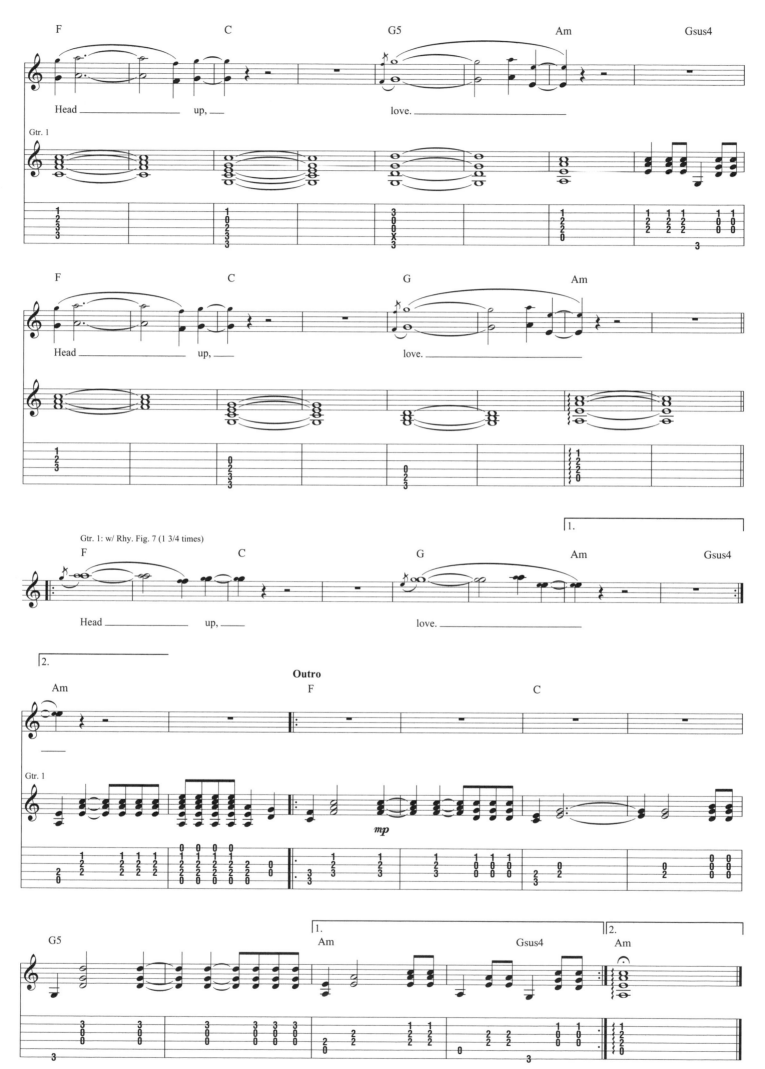

from The Last Bison - *Inheritance*

Switzerland

Words and Music by Ben Hardesty

Open E tuning:
(low to high) E-B-E-G#-B-E

Intro
Moderately ♩ = 118

*Chord symbols reflect implied harmony.

1. We

Verse

tried to sleep up in the banks of snow, __ but soon dis-cov-ered it was far too cold. __
drinks were hard-ly worth the price we paid, __ but we thanked God for them an-y-way. __ And

So we then re-treat-ed in-to town __ to find a place where there was lev-el ground. } Ah, __
with five min-utes left, we broke our backs to spend more mon-ey than eith-er of us had. __ }

Pre-Chorus

__ ah, __ ah, __ ah, __ call __ home. __ Doh, __

have you as a friend. ___ I'm pray-in' it was not at all pre-tend. ___

___ I need you ___ now ___ to help pick ___ me up from off the ground. ___

Interlude
Gtr. 1: w/ Riff A

2. Our

Interlude
Slower ♩ = 71

let ring

let ring

Rhy. Fig. 2

let ring

let ring

End Rhy. Fig. 2

194

Violin Solo

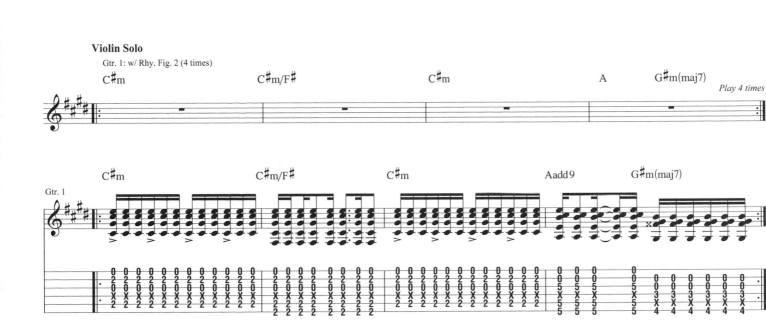

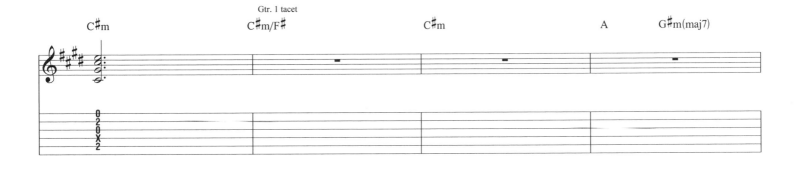

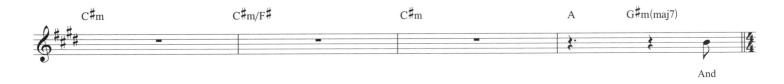

And

Chorus
Tempo I

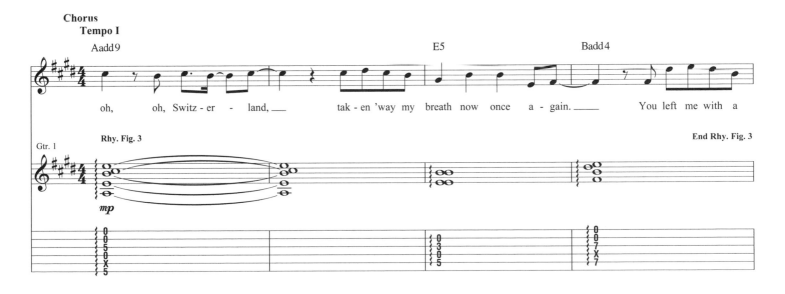

oh, oh, Switz - er - land, ___ tak - en 'way my breath now once a - gain. ___ You left me with a

sense of com - pas - sion ___ for the ones ___ who can't pick _ them - selves up off the ground. ___

Oh, Switz - er - land, ___ I nev - er thought I'd have you as a friend. ___ I'm pray - in' it was

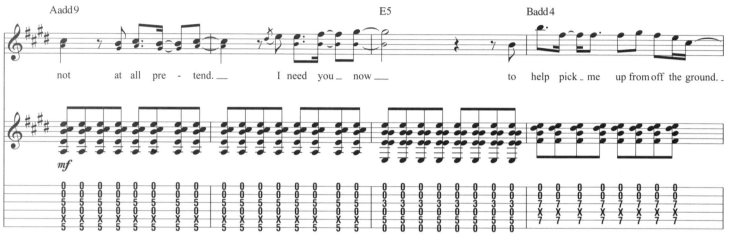

not at all pre - tend. ___ I need you ___ now ___ to help pick ___ me up from off the ground. ___

Oh, Switz - er - land, ___ you've tak - en 'way my breath now once a - gain. ___ You left me with a

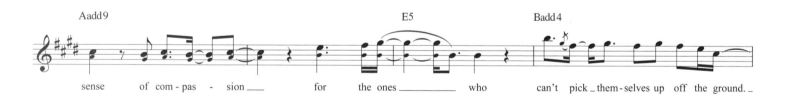

sense of com - pas - sion ___ for the ones ___ who can't pick ___ them - selves up off the ground. ___

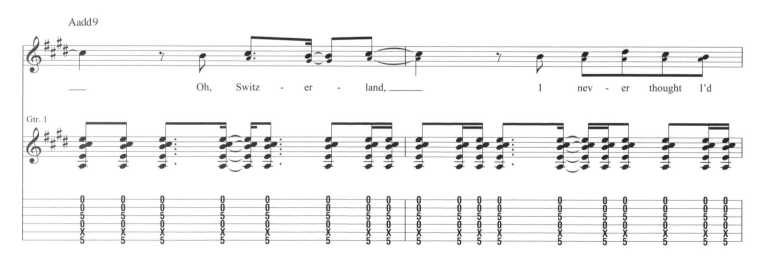

___ Oh, Switz - er - land, ___ I nev - er thought I'd

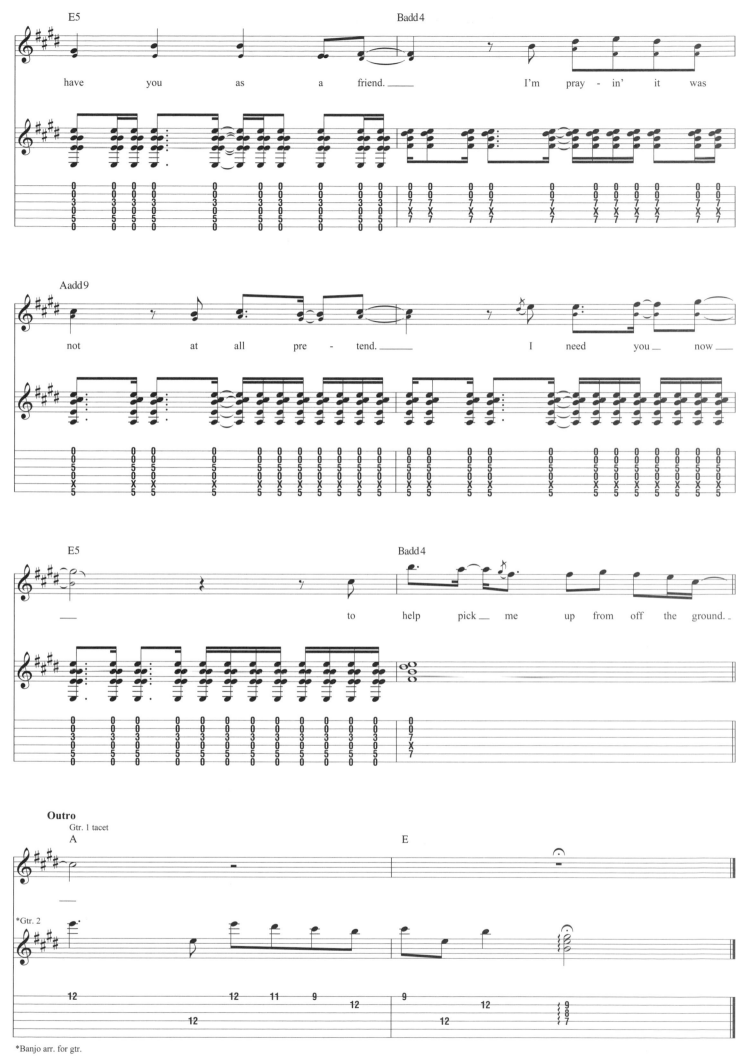

from Old Crow Medicine Show - *O.C.M.S.*

Take 'Em Away

Written by Critter Fuqua

Capo II

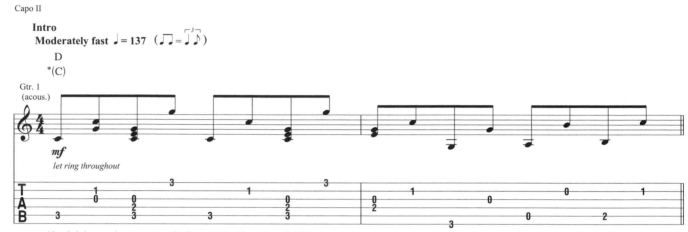

*Symbols in parentheses represent chord names respective to capoed guitar.
Symbols above reflect actual sounding chords. Capoed fret is "0" in tab.

Chorus

Take 'em a - way, _ take 'em a - way, _ Lord. _ Take a - way these chains _

_ from me. _ My heart is brok - en 'cause my _ spir - it's not _ free.

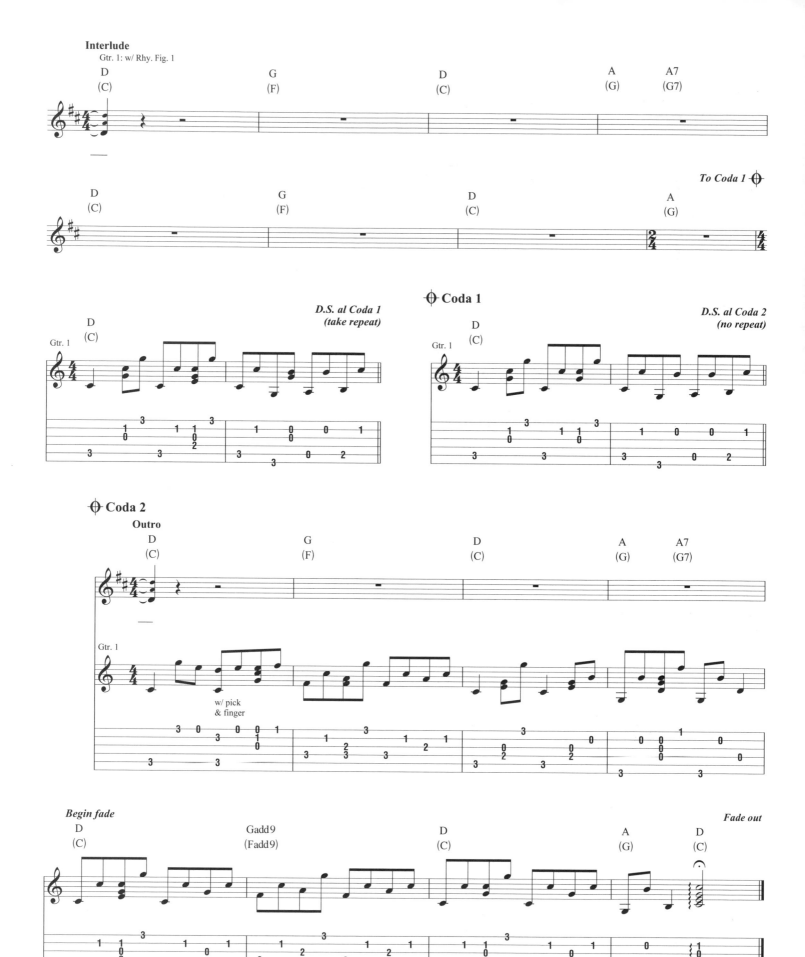

Additional lyrics

4. Land that I love is the land that I'm workin'
   But it's hard to love it all the time when your back is a, hurtin'.
   Gettin' too old now to push this here plow.
   Please let me lay down so I can look at the clouds.

5. Land that I know is where two rivers collide.
   The Brazos, the Navaso and the big blue sky.
   Flood plains, freight trains, watermelon vines,
   Of any place on God's green earth, this is where I choose to die.

Wagon Wheel

Words and Music by Bob Dylan and Ketch Secor

*Symbols in parentheses represent chord names respective to capoed guitar.
Symbols above reflect actual sounding chords. Capoed fret is "0" in tab.

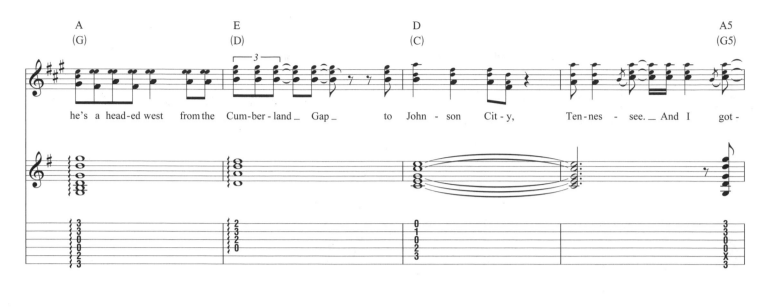

he's a head-ed west from the Cum-ber-land _ Gap _ to John-son Cit-y, Ten-nes - see. _ And I got-

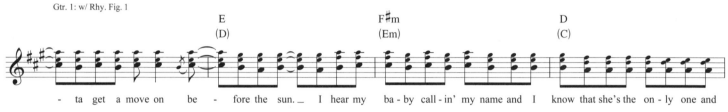

Gtr. 1: w/ Rhy. Fig. 1

- ta get a move on be - fore the sun. _ I hear my ba-by call-in' my name and I know that she's the on-ly one and

D.S. al Coda

if I die in Ral-eigh, least ___ I will __ die free. _____ So ___ rock _

⊕ Coda

___ me.

Gtr. 1

Gtr. 2

GUITAR NOTATION LEGEND

Guitar music can be notated three different ways: on a *musical staff*, in *tablature*, and in *rhythm slashes*.

RHYTHM SLASHES are written above the staff. Strum chords in the rhythm indicated. Use the chord diagrams found at the top of the first page of the transcription for the appropriate chord voicings. Round noteheads indicate single notes.

THE MUSICAL STAFF shows pitches and rhythms and is divided by bar lines into measures. Pitches are named after the first seven letters of the alphabet.

TABLATURE graphically represents the guitar fingerboard. Each horizontal line represents a string, and each number represents a fret.

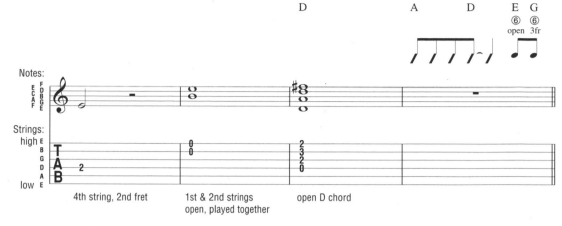

4th string, 2nd fret   1st & 2nd strings open, played together   open D chord

Definitions for Special Guitar Notation

HALF-STEP BEND: Strike the note and bend up 1/2 step.

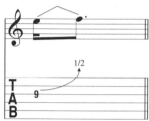

WHOLE-STEP BEND: Strike the note and bend up one step.

GRACE NOTE BEND: Strike the note and immediately bend up as indicated.

SLIGHT (MICROTONE) BEND: Strike the note and bend up 1/4 step.

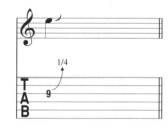

BEND AND RELEASE: Strike the note and bend up as indicated, then release back to the original note. Only the first note is struck.

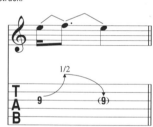

PRE-BEND: Bend the note as indicated, then strike it.

PRE-BEND AND RELEASE: Bend the note as indicated. Strike it and release the bend back to the original note.

UNISON BEND: Strike the two notes simultaneously and bend the lower note up to the pitch of the higher.

VIBRATO: The string is vibrated by rapidly bending and releasing the note with the fretting hand.

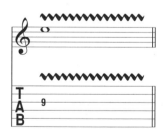

WIDE VIBRATO: The pitch is varied to a greater degree by vibrating with the fretting hand.

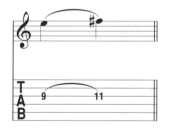

HAMMER-ON: Strike the first (lower) note with one finger, then sound the higher note (on the same string) with another finger by fretting it without picking.

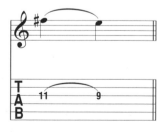

PULL-OFF: Place both fingers on the notes to be sounded. Strike the first note and without picking, pull the finger off to sound the second (lower) note.

LEGATO SLIDE: Strike the first note and then slide the same fret-hand finger up or down to the second note. The second note is not struck.

SHIFT SLIDE: Same as legato slide, except the second note is struck.

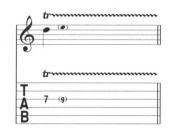

TRILL: Very rapidly alternate between the notes indicated by continuously hammering on and pulling off.

TAPPING: Hammer ("tap") the fret indicated with the pick-hand index or middle finger and pull off to the note fretted by the fret hand.

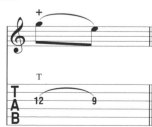

NATURAL HARMONIC: Strike the note while the fret-hand lightly touches the string directly over the fret indicated.

PINCH HARMONIC: The note is fretted normally and a harmonic is produced by adding the edge of the thumb or the tip of the index finger of the pick hand to the normal pick attack.

HARP HARMONIC: The note is fretted normally and a harmonic is produced by gently resting the pick hand's index finger directly above the indicated fret (in parentheses) while the pick hand's thumb or pick assists by plucking the appropriate string.

PICK SCRAPE: The edge of the pick is rubbed down (or up) the string, producing a scratchy sound.

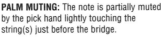

MUFFLED STRINGS: A percussive sound is produced by laying the fret hand across the string(s) without depressing, and striking them with the pick hand.

PALM MUTING: The note is partially muted by the pick hand lightly touching the string(s) just before the bridge.

RAKE: Drag the pick across the strings indicated with a single motion.

TREMOLO PICKING: The note is picked as rapidly and continuously as possible.

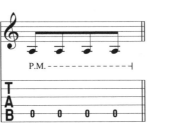

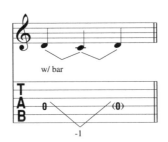

ARPEGGIATE: Play the notes of the chord indicated by quickly rolling them from bottom to top.

VIBRATO BAR DIVE AND RETURN: The pitch of the note or chord is dropped a specified number of steps (in rhythm), then returned to the original pitch.

VIBRATO BAR SCOOP: Depress the bar just before striking the note, then quickly release the bar.

VIBRATO BAR DIP: Strike the note and then immediately drop a specified number of steps, then release back to the original pitch.

Additional Musical Definitions

(accent) • Accentuate note (play it louder).

(accent) • Accentuate note with great intensity.

(staccato) • Play the note short.

 • Downstroke

V • Upstroke

D.S. al Coda • Go back to the sign (%), then play until the measure marked "*To Coda*," then skip to the section labelled "**Coda**."

D.C. al Fine • Go back to the beginning of the song and play until the measure marked "*Fine*" (end).

Rhy. Fig. • Label used to recall a recurring accompaniment pattern (usually chordal).

Riff • Label used to recall composed, melodic lines (usually single notes) which recur.

Fill • Label used to identify a brief melodic figure which is to be inserted into the arrangement.

Rhy. Fill • A chordal version of a Fill.

tacet • Instrument is silent (drops out).

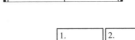
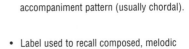 • Repeat measures between signs.

 • When a repeated section has different endings, play the first ending only the first time and the second ending only the second time.

NOTE: Tablature numbers in parentheses mean:
1. The note is being sustained over a system (note in standard notation is tied), or
2. The note is sustained, but a new articulation (such as a hammer-on, pull-off, slide or vibrato) begins, or
3. The note is a barely audible "ghost" note (note in standard notation is also in parentheses).

GUITAR RECORDED VERSIONS®

Guitar Recorded Versions® are note-for-note transcriptions of guitar music taken directly off recordings. This series, one of the most popular in print today, features some of the greatest guitar players and groups from blues and rock to country and jazz.

Guitar Recorded Versions are transcribed by the best transcribers in the business. Every book contains notes and tablature. Visit **www.halleonard.com** for our complete selection.

AUTHENTIC TRANSCRIPTIONS WITH NOTES AND TABLATURE

00690169	Eric Johnson – Venus Isle $22.95
00122439	Jack Johnson – From Here to Now to You $22.99
00690846	Jack Johnson and Friends – Sing-A-Longs and Lullabies for the Film Curious George $19.95
00690271	Robert Johnson – The New Transcriptions $24.95
00699131	Best of Janis Joplin $19.95
00690427	Best of Judas Priest $22.99
00690277	Best of Kansas $19.95
00690911	Best of Phil Keaggy $24.99
00690727	Toby Keith Guitar Collection $19.95
00120814	Killswitch Engage – Disarm the Descent $22.99
00690504	Very Best of Albert King $19.95
00690444	B.B. King & Eric Clapton – Riding with the King $22.99
00690134	Freddie King Collection $19.95
00691062	Kings of Leon – Come Around Sundown $22.99
00690157	Kiss – Alive! $19.95
00690356	Kiss – Alive II $22.99
00694903	Best of Kiss for Guitar $24.95
00690355	Kiss – Destroyer $16.95
14026320	Mark Knopfler – Get Lucky $22.99
00690164	Mark Knopfler Guitar – Vol. 1 ...... $19.95
00690163	Mark Knopfler/Chet Atkins – Neck and Neck $19.95
00690780	Korn – Greatest Hits, Volume 1 ...... $22.95
00690377	Kris Kristofferson Collection $19.95
00690834	Lamb of God – Ashes of the Wake $19.95
00690875	Lamb of God – Sacrament $19.95
00690977	Ray LaMontagne – Gossip in the Grain $19.99
00690823	Ray LaMontagne – Trouble $19.95
00691057	Ray LaMontagne and the Pariah Dogs – God Willin' & The Creek Don't Rise $22.99
00690781	Linkin Park – Hybrid Theory $22.95
00690782	Linkin Park – Meteora $22.95
00690922	Linkin Park – Minutes to Midnight $19.95
00699623	The Best of Chuck Loeb $19.95
00114563	The Lumineers $22.99
00690525	Best of George Lynch $24.99
00690955	Lynyrd Skynyrd – All-Time Greatest Hits $19.99
00694954	New Best of Lynyrd Skynyrd $19.95
00690577	Yngwie Malmsteen – Anthology $24.95
00690754	Marilyn Manson – Lest We Forget $19.95
00694956	Bob Marley – Legend $19.95
00690548	Very Best of Bob Marley & The Wailers – One Love $22.99
00694945	Bob Marley – Songs of Freedom $24.95
00690914	Maroon 5 – It Won't Be Soon Before Long $19.95
00690657	Maroon 5 – Songs About Jane $19.95
00690748	Maroon 5 – 1.22.03 Acoustic $19.95
00690989	Mastodon – Crack the Skye $22.99
00119220	Brent Mason – Hot Wired $19.99
00691176	Mastodon – The Hunter $22.99
00137718	Mastodon – Once More 'Round the Sun $22.99
00690616	Matchbox Twenty – More Than You Think You Are $19.95
00690239	Matchbox 20 – Yourself or Someone like You $19.95
00691942	Andy McKee – Art of Motion $22.99
00691034	Andy McKee – Joyland $19.99
00120080	The Don McLean Songbook $19.95
00694952	Megadeth – Countdown to Extinction $22.95
00690244	Megadeth – Cryptic Writings $19.95
00694951	Megadeth – Rust in Peace $22.95
00690011	Megadeth – Youthanasia $19.95
00690505	John Mellencamp Guitar Collection $19.95
00690562	Pat Metheny – Bright Size Life $19.95
00691073	Pat Metheny with Christian McBride & Antonion Sanchez – Day Trip/Tokyo Day Trip Live ... $22.99
00690646	Pat Metheny – One Quiet Night $19.95
00690559	Pat Metheny – Question & Answer $19.95
00118836	Pat Metheny – Unity Band $22.99
00102590	Pat Metheny – What's It All About $22.99
00690040	Steve Miller Band Greatest Hits $19.95
00119338	Ministry Guitar Tab Collection $24.99
00690769	Modest Mouse – Good News for People Who Love Bad News $19.95
00102591	Wes Montgomery Guitar Anthology $24.99
00694802	Gary Moore – Still Got the Blues $22.99
00691005	Best of Motion City Soundtrack $19.99
00690787	Mudvayne – L.D. 50 ...... $22.95
00691070	Mumford & Sons – Sigh No More $22.99
00118196	Muse – The 2nd Law $19.99
00690996	My Morning Jacket Collection $19.99
00690984	Matt Nathanson – Some Mad Hope $22.99
00690611	Nirvana $22.95
00694895	Nirvana – Bleach $19.95

00694913	Nirvana – In Utero $19.95
00694883	Nirvana – Nevermind $19.95
00690026	Nirvana – Unplugged in New York $19.95
00120112	No Doubt – Tragic Kingdom $22.95
00690226	Oasis – The Other Side of Oasis $19.95
00307163	Oasis – Time Flies... 1994-2009 ...... $19.99
00690818	The Best of Opeth $22.95
00691052	Roy Orbison – Black & White Night $22.95
00694847	Best of Ozzy Osbourne $22.95
00690399	Ozzy Osbourne – The Ozzman Cometh $22.99
00690129	Ozzy Osbourne – Ozzmosis $22.95
00690933	Best of Brad Paisley $22.95
00690995	Brad Paisley – Play: The Guitar Album $24.99
00690939	Christopher Parkening – Solo Pieces $19.95
00690594	Best of Les Paul $19.95
00694855	Pearl Jam – Ten $22.95
00690439	A Perfect Circle – Mer De Noms $19.95
00690725	Best of Carl Perkins $19.95
00690499	Tom Petty – Definitive Guitar Collection $19.95
00690868	Tom Petty – Highway Companion $19.95
00690176	Phish – Billy Breathes $22.95
00691249	Phish – Junta $22.99
00690428	Pink Floyd – Dark Side of the Moon $19.95
00690789	Best of Poison $19.95
00690299	Best of Elvis: The King of Rock 'n' Roll $19.95
00692535	Elvis Presley $19.95
00690925	The Very Best of Prince $22.99
00690003	Classic Queen $24.95
00694975	Queen – Greatest Hits $24.95
00690670	Very Best of Queensryche $19.95
00690878	The Raconteurs – Broken Boy Soldiers $19.95
00109303	Radiohead Guitar Anthology $24.99
00694910	Rage Against the Machine $19.95
00119834	Rage Against the Machine – Guitar Anthology $22.99
00690179	Rancid – And Out Come the Wolves $22.95
00690426	Best of Ratt $19.95
00690055	Red Hot Chili Peppers – Blood Sugar Sex Magik $19.95
00690584	Red Hot Chili Peppers – By the Way $19.95
00690379	Red Hot Chili Peppers – Californication $19.95
00690673	Red Hot Chili Peppers – Greatest Hits $19.95
00690090	Red Hot Chili Peppers – One Hot Minute $22.95
00691166	Red Hot Chili Peppers – I'm with You $22.99
00690852	Red Hot Chili Peppers – Stadium Arcadium $24.95
00690511	Django Reinhardt – The Definitive Collection $19.95
00690779	Relient K – MMHMM $19.95
00690643	Relient K – Two Lefts Don't Make a Right ... But Three Do $19.95
00690260	Jimmie Rodgers Guitar Collection $19.95
14041901	Rodrigo Y Gabriela and C.U.B.A. – Area 52 ...... $24.99
00690014	Rolling Stones – Exile on Main Street $24.95
00690631	Rolling Stones – Guitar Anthology $27.95
00690685	David Lee Roth – Eat 'Em and Smile $19.95
00690031	Santana's Greatest Hits $19.95
00690796	Very Best of Michael Schenker $19.95
00690566	Best of Scorpions $22.95
00690604	Bob Seger – Guitar Anthology $22.99
00691012	Shadows Fall – Retribution $22.99
00690803	Best of Kenny Wayne Shepherd Band $19.95
00690750	Kenny Wayne Shepherd – The Place You're In $19.95
00690857	Shinedown – Us and Them $19.95
00122218	Skillet – Rise $22.99
00690872	Slayer – Christ Illusion $19.95
00690813	Slayer – Guitar Collection $19.95
00690419	Slipknot $19.95
00690973	Slipknot – All Hope Is Gone $22.99
00690330	Social Distortion – Live at the Roxy $19.95
00120004	Best of Steely Dan $24.95
00694921	Best of Steppenwolf $22.95
00690655	Best of Mike Stern $19.95
14041588	Cat Stevens – Tea for the Tillerman $19.99
00690949	Rod Stewart Guitar Anthology $19.95
00690021	Sting – Fields of Gold $19.95
00690520	Styx Guitar Collection $19.95
00120081	Sublime $19.95
00690992	Sublime – Robbin' the Hood $19.99
00690519	SUM 41 – All Killer No Filler $19.95
00691072	Best of Supertramp $22.99
00690994	Taylor Swift $22.99
00690993	Taylor Swift – Fearless $22.99
00115957	Taylor Swift – Red $21.99
00691063	Taylor Swift – Speak Now $22.99
00690767	Switchfoot – The Beautiful Letdown $19.95
00690531	System of a Down – Toxicity $19.95

AUTHENTIC TRANSCRIPTIONS
WITH NOTES AND TABLATURE

00694824	Best of James Taylor $17.99
00694887	Best of Thin Lizzy $19.95
00690871	Three Days Grace – One-X $19.95
00690891	30 Seconds to Mars – A Beautiful Lie $19.95
00690233	The Merle Travis Collection $19.99
00690683	Robin Trower – Bridge of Sighs $19.95
00699191	U2 – Best of: 1980-1990 ...... $19.95
00690732	U2 – Best of: 1990-2000 ...... $19.95
00690894	U2 – 18 Singles $19.95
00690039	Steve Vai – Alien Love Secrets $24.95
00690172	Steve Vai – Fire Garden $24.95
00660137	Steve Vai – Passion & Warfare $24.95
00690881	Steve Vai – Real Illusions: Reflections $24.95
00694904	Steve Vai – Sex and Religion $24.95
00110385	Steve Vai – The Story of Light $22.99
00690392	Steve Vai – The Ultra Zone $19.95
00700555	Van Halen – Van Halen $19.99
00690024	Stevie Ray Vaughan – Couldn't Stand the Weather $19.95
00690370	Stevie Ray Vaughan and Double Trouble – The Real Deal: Greatest Hits Volume 2 ...... $22.95
00690116	Stevie Ray Vaughan – Guitar Collection $24.95
00660136	Stevie Ray Vaughan – In Step $19.95
00694879	Stevie Ray Vaughan – In the Beginning $19.95
00660058	Stevie Ray Vaughan – Lightnin' Blues '83-'87 ...... $24.95
00690036	Stevie Ray Vaughan – Live Alive $24.95
00694835	Stevie Ray Vaughan – The Sky Is Crying $22.95
00690025	Stevie Ray Vaughan – Soul to Soul $19.95
00690015	Stevie Ray Vaughan – Texas Flood $19.95
00690772	Velvet Revolver – Contraband $22.95
00109770	Volbeat Guitar Collection $22.99
00121808	Volbeat – Outlaw Gentlemen & Shady Ladies $22.99
00690132	The T-Bone Walker Collection $19.95
00694789	Muddy Waters – Deep Blues $24.95
00690071	Weezer (The Blue Album) $19.95
00690516	Weezer (The Green Album) $19.95
00690286	Weezer – Pinkerton $19.95
00691046	Weezer – Rarities Edition $22.99
00117511	Whitesnake Guitar Collection $19.99
00690447	Best of the Who $24.95
00691941	The Who – Acoustic Guitar Collection $22.99
00691006	Wilco Guitar Collection $22.99
00690672	Best of Dar Williams $19.95
00691017	Wolfmother – Cosmic Egg $22.99
00690319	Stevie Wonder – Some of the Best $17.95
00690596	Best of the Yardbirds $19.95
00690844	Yellowcard – Lights and Sounds $19.95
00690916	The Best of Dwight Yoakam $19.95
00691020	Neil Young – After the Goldrush $22.99
00691019	Neil Young – Everybody Knows This Is Nowhere $19.95
00690904	Neil Young – Harvest $29.99
00691021	Neil Young – Harvest Moon $22.99
00690905	Neil Young – Rust Never Sleeps $19.95
00690443	Frank Zappa – Hot Rats $19.95
00690624	Frank Zappa and the Mothers of Invention – One Size Fits All $22.99
00690623	Frank Zappa – Over-Nite Sensation $22.99
00121684	ZZ Top – Early Classics $24.99
00690589	ZZ Top – Guitar Anthology $24.95
00690960	ZZ Top Guitar Classics $19.99

HAL•LEONARD® CORPORATION

7777 W. BLUEMOUND RD. P.O. BOX 13819 MILWAUKEE, WI 53213

Complete songlists and more at **www.halleonard.com**

Prices, contents, and availability subject to change without notice.

1214